# The Year's Work in Medievalism

## Edited by Gwendolyn A. Morgan

*XVIII*
*2003*

Wipf & Stock Publishers
Eugene, Oregon

# The Year's Work in Medievalism
Series Editor, Gwendolyn Morgan

*The Year's Work in Medievalism*, volume XVIII, is based upon but not restricted to the 2003 proceedings of the Annual International Conference on Medievalism, organized by the Director of Conferences of *Studies in Medievalism*, and, for 2003, Tom Shippey. *The Year's Work in Medievalism* also publishes bibliographies, book reviews, and announcements of conferences and other events.

The 2003 volume is indexed in *The Modern Language Association International Bibliography*.

Copyright © *Studies in Medievalism* 2004
ISSN 0899-3106
ISBN 1-59244-745-7

All rights reserved. Except as permitted under current legislation, no part of this work may be photocopied, stored in a retrieval system, published, transmitted, or reproduced in any form or by any means without the prior permission of the copyright owner.

First published in 2004 by Wipf and Stock Publishers
199 West 8th Ave., Suite 3
Eugene, OR 97401
http://www.wipfandstock.com/Publish.htm
for *Studies in Medievalism*

*The Year's Work in Medievalism* is an imprint of *Studies in Medievalism*. For the series, generally, write Gwendolyn Morgan, Editor, *The Year's Work in Medievalism,* Department of English, Montana State University, Bozeman, MT 59717.

*The Year's Work in Medievalism*
Volume XVIII 2003

Gwendolyn A. Morgan, Introduction: Medievalism and
    the Creation of Identity      1 – 4

Anne Thornton, Romancing a Romantic: The *Lais* of
    Marie de France and Certain Keatsian Odes      5 – 19

Edward L. Risden, Tolkien, Ricoeur, and Eliot:
    The World of the Text and the 20th-Century Wasteland      20 – 25

James R. Keller, The Power of his Horror: Abjection
    and Macbeth      26 – 33

Peter G. Christensen, Searching for God and Arthur:
    Jim Hunter's *Percival and the Presence of God*      34 – 46

Grace Chiu Chan, The Medievalism of Kantorowicz:
    *Bildung,* Jewish Identity, and National Socialism      47 – 65

Marjon Ames, Reigning Arthur In: Mythological
    Appropriation and the English Monarchy      66 – 76

Robert Sirabian, Anglo-Saxonism and Charles Kingsley's
    *Hereward the Wake: Last of the English*.      77 – 90

List of Participants in the 18th International Conference
    on Medievalism      91 – 93

## Introduction: Medievalism and the Creation of Identity

### Gwendolyn A. Morgan

The essays in *The Year's Work in Medievalism: 2002* deal primarily with the use of the ideals, myths, and historical figures of the Middle Ages in establishing identity, whether at the personal, political, or national level. It thus represents a chance to revisit one of Umberto Eco's primary claims in his seminal work of medievalism, *Travels in Hyperreality*. While Eco asserted that the medieval period represents the "infancy" of the modern age, and hence explains our continued penchant for returning to them as attempts to understand who we are, the contributors to the present volume find much earlier instances of its importance to the Western sense of self. Thus, not only twentieth-century quests for identity, but various others from the twelfth through the nineteenth centuries are investigated in the individual essays.

The most fertile ground for medievalism to function still lies in fiction and poetry, and so the collection begins with Anne Thornton's essay on the influence of certain lais by Marie de France on several of Keats' important odes. Although the poet himself never acknowledged Marie's influence, suggestions in letters and personal papers, as well as appropriations of Marie's imagery and plot lines too stark to deny, indicate that Keats found a kinship with Marie in their common attempt to be "anonymous," allowing their poems to stand on their own, creator-less as it were. In other words, Marie was a Romantic before her time, and in her Keats discovered early intimations of Romantic ideas of the imagination and the primacy of art, along with his personal conviction that the poet is secondary to it. Thus, in Marie's medieval poetry, Keats finds confirmation of his own identity as poet.

Such a stance, of course, appears to foreshadow Tolkien's theory of sub-creation, where the tales, images, and persons of fantasy and myth already exist somewhere and merely await the poet or storyteller's art to give them form and existence. The essay which follows, then, Edward Risden's treatment of Wasteland imagery in Tolkien and Eliot, touches upon Tolkien's conviction (expressed in his essay "On Faerie Tales") that the act of sub-creation through fiction allows more than an escape from the real world; it offers us a means by which to re-shape and improve the Wasteland of our actual present. Risden examines how Tolkien's own fiction fulfills his theory, along with the Tolkien's stated aim of creating a mythology for England and thereby a cohesive English national identity. By comparing it to T.S. Eliot's use of medieval Wasteland imagery as an allegory for the early twentieth century, he elucidates the very different conclusions reached and effects created by the two authors.

With James Keller's essay on abjection in Shakespeare's *Macbeth*, we move from the creation of actual identity through fiction to creation (and destruction) of the individual sense of self within the fiction. The much noted disunity in the title character, Keller claims, is actually an accurate depiction of abjection in Macbeth, brought on by his own divided conscience. What the essay adds in particular to the present collection is that Macbeth's sense of self, of honor, and of cosmic order relies on his acceptance of the medieval world view; within that world view, the cosmic laws which Macbeth transgresses with his murders and attempted usurpation of the throne demand the resultant (and corresponding) disorder within his own psyche. In other words, Shakespeare creates an identity for Macbeth based upon medieval concepts which, in the author's own time, are quickly becoming obsolete. Moreover, Keller adds to existing work devoted to Shakespeare's conservative adherence to medieval cosmology and its religious and moral implications discovered by scholars in other of Shakespeare's plays.

In contrast to Macbeth's situation, where personal identity relies upon the external world, that examined by Peter Christensen, in his treatment of Jim Hunter's *Percival and the Presence of God*, finds the medieval myth of the grail quest adapted to an existential philosophy. Like Eliot and Tolkien, Hunter's novel emphasizes Wasteland imagery, here a metaphor for the hero's psychological condition. Percival, rather than seeing himself as participating in the larger quest of Arthur's knights, finds himself doubting even the existence of Arthur and his court, because his own experience and feelings have not shown them to be true. Moreover, as Christensen points out, even Percival's perception of God and the holiness of the grail is shaped only by his internal sense that they must be so, not by any external proofs or assertions by others. In this way, Hunter has all but stood the medieval myth, where the individual is ultimately absorbed by the divine, on its head.

With Grace Chan's examination of Ernst Kantorowicz's life and canon, we leave the worlds of sub-creation and move outward to what Tolkien would call primary reality. Forced by the growth of Nazi power and idealism to confront the dichotomy of his identity as German Jew, Kantorowicz looks back to the medieval emperor Frederick II, who, he believed, "was capable of transcending such fragmentation by combining contradictions into a syncretistic whole," while apparently ignoring Frederick's stigmatizing of the Jews of his own empire. However, such was, Chan points out, the idealism of a young man in the 1920s; by the close of his career, after the misappropriation of his work in the Nazi cause, flight from his homeland, and disillusionment with another irrational nationalism during the McCarthy era, Kantorowicz abandons his earlier attempts to reconcile the two halves of his own—and Germany's—"spiritual bifurcation." Even so, he returns to medieval philosophy in the theory of "body corporeal/body mystical" to take his attempt to resolve the dichotomy to the higher level of the human condition—the identity of the human race.

Marjon Ames addresses a similar subject in her examination of the late medieval and early modern monarchs of England, whose appropriation of the mythical King Arthur and the purported trappings and practices of his Camelot provided justification for their own claims to the throne. Ames traces Arthur's regal influence from Henry II to Elizabeth I, providing a survey of the various ways in which they did so. What makes the present essay important are previously unevaluated links to the survival and yet absorption of Welsh national identity into that of the English; the legacy of Arthurian identification as a coherent, virtually uninterrupted practice dating back to Gerald of Wales and Geoffrey of Monmouth; and Ames' examination of why the practice waned under Henry VIII and disappeared with the ascension of Elizabeth.

Returning once again to the issue of medievalism and the creation of national identity, Robert Sirabian discovers in the title character of Charles Kingsley's *Hereward the Wake: Last of the English* the same kind of "spiritual bifurcation" which Chan finds dominating Kantorowicz's sense of personal and national identity. Kingsley's novel, however, gives us a hero who is seemingly unaware (most of the time) of his own divided identity, a result, according to Sirabian, of the double Victorian vision of the Anglo-Saxons. At once embracing a heroic and decidedly English past, and rejecting primitive, barbaric forbears who clash with the Victorian ideal of history as progress, the age produced primarily fiction advancing one or the other perception. On occasion some authors (Walter Scott is Sirabian's case in point) attempted to derive a national identity from both Anglo-Saxon and Norman strains, showing the possibility of a peaceful co-existence of the ilk which the end of *Ivanhoe* evokes. In this sense, Scott, Kingsley, and others like them foreshadow Tolkien's fiction, where the various cultures of early England—Celtic, Anglo-Saxon, Norman-French—find representation in the various races of Middle Earth. However, unlike his contemporary compatriots, Kingsley finds destruction of Anglo-Saxon society as necessary and laudable, and at the same time representing irrecoverable loss of heroic freedoms and virtues. In this, he alone of his age comes close to Tolkien and his sense that the destruction of the Ring of Power also necessitates the passing of the elves and wizards from this world. Kingsley thus leaves us with a constructed English identity, but one that is forever divided in itself, both success and failure at the same time.

What all these perspectives, individually and collectively, demonstrate is that any definition of identity is slippery at best. How can one separate personal identity from national and ethnic membership? Moreover, how can ethnic or national identity be anything but at best splintered, given the history of Western nations over the last millennia or two? How many ethnic groups can claim undiluted heritage? Perhaps it is the desire for a definitive oneness in the face of such realizations that underlies the impulse to return to the medieval period to answer to the question of who we are, for in the popular vision of the Middle Ages since (at least) the fifteenth century, that oneness seemed to exist. Even though we now know this not to have been the case, that the Middle Ages have been deliberately manipulated in propaganda by monarchs, dictators, and democratic leaders; unconsciously used as frameworks to define the individual and justify his actions; that they have survived a vast array of changes in political, religious, and psychological theories; all are proof of how deeply we have internalized them and how powerful they remain in our sense of reality.

*MONTANA STATE UNIVERSITY—BOZEMAN*

# Romancing a Romantic:
## The *Lais* of Marie de France and Certain Keatsian Odes

### Anne Thornton

Much has been ably written and dutifully re-written by twentieth- and twenty-first century scholars concerning Keats's poetic resemblance to Dryden, Spenser (at least in his eighteenth-century guise), Shakespeare, and even quite recently to a mysterious Richard Roos masquerading as Chaucer.[1] Comparatively little source study has been focused on the possibly unmediated influence of medieval romance—unmediated, that is, save by translation and time—upon Keats's poetry and particularly his odes. No doubt the chief reason for neglecting the tapestry of possible non-Chaucerian medieval references as a backdrop for chameleon Keatsian poetics[2] is one apparently irrefutable fact: aside from the works of Chaucer, no truly medieval texts are known to have been in the poet's possession. Thus, speculation may easily run amok. Even so, "a Question," to Keats, "is the best beacon towards a little Speculation" (I.175). If one is to contemplate possible medieval sources, few candidates are as congenial to Keats's notion of the identity-less poet (I.387) as Marie de France, who quite literally has no existence outside of a vague self-identification in the prologue to her *Lais* and another in the Harley manuscript's prologue to *Guigemar*.[3]

Although Keats had no patience with contemporary bluestockings, he admired female literary genius at a sufficiently safe historical distance; he was enamored of at least one female poet of the Renaissance, the "'matchless Orinda'" (that is, Katherine Fowler Philips), whose Donne-like verse "To Mrs. M. A. at Parting" he quoted in its entirety in an 1817 letter to J. H. Reynolds with enthusiastic approbation for her "delicate fancy" (I.163-65). Of course, Marie predates Philips by nearly five hundred years, but the centuries may easily be forgotten if one realizes that she shared Keats's catalytic vision of the poetic calling—the conviction that the poet is "continually...filling some other body" (I.387)—that is missing from the detached witticisms of "To Mrs. M. A." While Keats and Marie were not mere redactors of extant texts, it is certain that neither was ashamed to borrow, and whatever they touched was typically transformed.[4] A more substantial argument in favor of this largely anonymous poet's possible literary influence may be based upon a surprising number of coincidental themes and images, as well as the necessary fact that her tales were available to Keats both in French and in translation, albeit usually in abbreviated form and not always in verse. Before reassessing several of Keats's odes and other lyrics as debtors to this obscurely illustrious twelfth-century Frenchwoman, however, some specifics regarding Keats's access to and incorporation of medieval texts in general—and French medieval romance in particular—as well as his possibly ambivalent attitude toward romance by the time of the odes' composition require elucidation.

I

Keats's library was understandably small, given his youth and slim financial resources, but its size does not preclude a certain remarkable fluidity capable of teasing scholars out of all thought. Charles Brown catalogued the poet's holdings at a mere eighty-one volumes at the time of his death,[5] but it is nearly impossible to account for the numerous books that were continually passing in and out of Keats's possession. An 1819 letter to his publishers Taylor and Hessey, in which the poet promises a return of an apparently substantial number of loans (II.111), titillates but ultimately frustrates with its omission of any definitive list of his borrowings. One volume Keats may have neglected to return—for it turns up in Richard Woodhouse's catalogue under the title "Dante's Inferno by Cary"—is the *Hell* volume of Henry Francis Cary's English translation (Keats did not at that time read Italian), published in its second edition in 1819.[6] Since no references are made in the letters to Dante either in English or Italian before 1820, it is unlikely that Keats possessed a volume before 1819. Thus, his borrowings might have been taking a medieval turn before the composition of his odes in that year—if not to obscure romances, at least to the *Divine Comedy*.

Keats was an habitual borrower from other sources as well, most of which are difficult or impossible to trace. He did, at some point in his career, obtain a reader's ticket to the British Museum under the auspices of Benjamin Haydon.[7] Although in April 1819 he admitted to being in debt for sums which "might have formed a library to my taste" (II.54), he amply supplied his literary wants from generous friends' bookshelves. A later letter finds him "dreaming over my Books or rather other peoples Books" (II.239).

Almost as important as a study of the poet's elusive reading habits is a recognition of the fact that whatever texts Keats did obtain were not merely read but "dreamed over." It is this Keatsian habit that should send scholars source-hunting in earnest, for the poet's dreams were probably, in keeping with his catalytic interpretation of the poet's calling, such stuff as his poetry was made of. Even Keats's conservative early twentieth-century biographer, Sir Sidney Colvin, suggests that the sonnet "How many bards" teases the reader into speculation about the "working of Keats's poetic reading" upon his fancy.[8]

There remains, of course, the question of exactly what took Keats's fancy. Except that the poet's letters indicate a life-long fascination with and absorption of things medieval, one might argue that such interest was confined to the period during which he wrote "La Belle Dame sans Merci," *The Eve of St.*

*Agnes, The Eve of St. Mark,* and *Isabella, or The Pot of Basil*: one of a chameleon artist's several changes of hue before attaining the sustained beauty and virtuosity of the 1819 odes. His letters admittedly refer most often to Chaucer, but there are also liberal sprinklings of references to Continental romances. What is curious is that the references are not formal, common-place book entries; instead, the poet insinuates them into the mundane recorded details of his life. His mind has worked its peculiar catalytic magic—it has fully assimilated material and immediately reinvented it for its own purposes. As early as 1817, Keats fancifully associates his money troubles with the motif of the knightly quest, claiming that a twenty-pound note is better protection against "that spring-headed Hydra the Dun" than a full suit of armor or "the aid of...Archimago or Urganda" (I.145-46). Juxtaposed with an expected Spenserian allusion is a reference to a character in the fifteenth-century Spanish romance *Amadis of Gaul*, apparently taken from fourteenth-century sources and originally a French tale. Keats was probably familiar with it via Robert Southey's popular abridged translation published in 1803. The reference is interesting, not only for its dramatization of the creative working of Keats's imagination upon a text, but also because it represents a tale not listed among the contents of the poet's library as catalogued by Woodhouse. It is clear, then, that Keats had read at least one quasi- or late-medieval romance not in his possession: thus it might be conjectured with some certainty that he had read others.

The "innate love of chivalry" Lowell observes in Keats[9] manifested itself more substantially than in the occasional epistolary witticism. From 1817 onward, his poetry frequently takes up the medieval thread, and among the allusions and sources French romance is amply represented, bringing him successively closer to Marie's *Lais*. Colvin, especially, has great faith in the breadth of Keats's French reading; he maintains that the poet "was more widely read in out-of-the-way French literature than could have been expected from his opportunities."[10] *Endymion*, according to Colvin, echoes a variety of both pseudo- and bona fide medieval texts, from *Endimion* by Gombauld ("a very wild and withal tiresome French seventeenth-century prose romance on Keats's own theme") to the early French *Sethos*, which was readily available under the title *Voyage d'Antènor* during the poet's lifetime.[11] Robert Gittings, borrowing from the unpublished notes of D. H. Walter, claims that *The Eve of St. Agnes* is colored by Keats's coincident reading of a romance trilogy written and collected by M. de Tressan entitled *Bibliothèque Universelle des Dames: Romans*.[12]

Given Keats's familiarity with and allusions to Continental romance, an acquaintance with the work of Marie de France may indeed be more than a speculative scholarly fantasy. The most telling evidence lies in a mere fragment of a narrative poem scribbled in the margins of his notes during a lecture at St. Thomas's Hospital. Colvin asserts that the piece "reads like the beginning of an attempt to tell the story of the Old French 'Lai d'Aristote' " which Keats may well have read in the eighteenth-century prose translation included in M. Le Grand's *Fabliaux au Contes* (1781) or in the Anglicized verse of G. L. Way's *Fabliaux or Tales* (1800).[13] In these volumes can also be found *Guigemar,* one of Marie's *Lais* which appears to have caught Keats's fancy. It requires but one speculative step further to suggest that Keats had also read at some time a popular anthology by the writer of the preface, notes, and appendix to Way's *Fabliaux,* namely *Specimens of Early English Metrical Romances* by George Ellis (1805). While the title may not appear very promising, the "Historical Introduction"—which ambitiously proposes to trace "The Rise and Progress of Romantic Composition in France and England" in the space of seventy-five pages—includes "abstracts" of nine of the *Lais*; the reader is referred to Le Grand and Way for *Guigemar* and *Lanval,* since they had been "faithfully analyzed by Le Grand and beautifully translated by Way [and require] no further notice in this place.".[14] The best source—the one in which both Way's and Ellis's translations and abstracts are represented in a single volume (the translations of *Chevrefoil* as "Sir Tristam" by Sir Walter Scott excepted)—was collected and edited by an obscure Matilda Betham in 1816, one year prior to the appearance of Keats's first epistolary medieval references.

## II

If, as has been generally accepted, Keats had by February 1818 (with the commencement of the writing of *Isabella*), opted in favor of anti-romance, any attempt to trace Marie's influence would be at best an exercise in uncovering a whole new set of texts that Keats may have cheerfully deconstructed. Those who espouse this theory invariably cite the *Lear* sonnet with its farewell to "golden-tongued Romance with serene lute" (1)[15] and address subsequent works as though undeniably composed in the same spirit. Jack Stillinger cogently argues the point with regard to *Isabella* in his 1968 article on the subject, but the case is weakened by Morris Dickstein's too-facile definition of romance as well as by Walter Jackson Bate's thorough 1963 study, in which he convincingly argues that "with it [*Isabella*], as with the other poems he had been writing since the new beginning three months ago [January 1818], he was only marking time."[16] The essentially second-rate status afforded the poem by most critics seems to corroborate this assessment.

Implicit in Dickstein's *Keats and His Poetry* is the notion of medieval romance as simplistic and relatively unconcerned with real human problems. Arming himself with the inevitable reference to *Lear*, Dickstein argues that the poet eschews escapism in his odes, "the first poems in which Keats fully acts upon the mission to which he consecrated himself [in *Lear*]: to put aside romance."[17] What is conveniently ignored is the fact that medieval romance as a genre is not always escapist and is notoriously difficult to define. Even the traditional categorizations—Matter of Britain, Matter of France, and Matter of Rome—embrace literature entirely outside the fairy-tale mode, as is evident from the last designation. Further, one medieval scholar has suggested the inclusion of a fourth, unorthodox category: "Matter of Breton," within which Marie's *Lais* would obviously fall.[18] Although Marie's tales are sprinkled with magical devices, they are not wholly dependent on them for interest or momentum of plot; in fact, they do not often stray far from the truth of the human heart. Readers of her tales seem inevitably to marvel at their emotional realism.[19] For instance, following a summary of the *Lais*, Martin Donovan, a critic particularly interested in the *lai* as a genre, claims that "any definition of the Breton lay...has to be broad enough to allow for both the realistic and the marvelous."[20] Even if the prevailing perception of Keats's change of attitude toward the typical romance is accurate, the *lai* provides him with a romantic sub-genre that is still magical—as are the post-1818 "La Belle Dame," *The Eve of St. Agnes*, and, as will be argued, some of the odes—but not necessarily simplistic and unrealistic in its approach to the human condition.

Yet nagging questions remain: even if the anomalous *Isabella* is set aside and ambiguities of genre are clarified, Keats's apparent disgust with "skyey knight errantry" in a January 1818 letter (I.209) and his puzzling "Epistle to J. H. Reynolds" in March of the same year must be addressed. In the case of the January epistle, the phrase appears to be less an evocation of the poet's literary opinion than a reaction to the web of social problems beginning to shape themselves into the vexing Woman Question of later decades. Likewise, the puzzling verse epistle to Reynolds may be regarded as "a series of ridiculous and fantastic dreams of romantic origin,"[21] but one might also read it as a foster-child of the medieval dream vision—is not *Piers Plowman*, to the uninitiated reader, seemingly just as phantasmagoric? As a dream vision, the poem might also be read as a prototype for "Ode to a Nightingale," where a like catalogue of impressions, also informed by romance, is neither "ridiculous" nor "fantastic."

Likewise, as the *Lear* sonnet is the lodestar of the anti-romance critics, it cannot be dismissed out of hand. Bate again illuminates the issue, though he does not clearly argue in defense of a persevering medievalistic impulse. The re-reading of Shakespeare's tragedy may have indeed represented "another beginning," but it was most clearly one in which "the play became increasingly a symbol of what he hoped ultimately to reach"[22]—that is, his desire to create a drama of Shakespearean quality.[23] Shakespeare's *King Lear* itself owes much to the realm of the fairy tale, albeit the plot is also invested with remarkable realism—as are Marie's *Lais*. One might, without injustice, draw a parallel between Keats's relative failure as a dramatist and his eventual inability to abandon romance entirely. It must be remembered that the poet who bid romance "adieu" in 1818 nonetheless addressed his beloved Fanny Brawne as "herte mine"—a phrase borrowed from Chaucer's *Troilus and Criseyde*—in October 1819, one month after he composed his final ode.[24] The chameleon once again evades the too-earnest scholar.

### III

Still, the speculative thread linking the shadowy twelfth-century romancer and the nineteenth-century Romantic might seem to be anchored only on negatives—particularly the absence of any evidence to the contrary—but such is not the case. In one of several futile escapist impulses in "Ode to a Nightingale," the poet describes the desired vintage never brewed as "tasting of...[d]ance, and Provençal song, and sunburnt mirth" (13, 14); further, he does not specifically reject that intoxicating lyricism, as he does the imagined wine itself, for the "Provençal song" might well be a feather in "viewless wings of Poesy" (33). Aside from this poetic reference, French poetry seemed to have gained a certain cachet among the members of the Keats circle: the poet's lawyer friend James Rice was, in 1819, "full of enthusiasm for Provençal poetry."[25] Keats's own Gallic interests were diffuse—ranging from the French romances mentioned above to troubadour poetry to the contents of a curious volume in his library entitled *Celtic Researches*, which, though primarily a linguistic treatise, might have linked in his mind French literature in general to the Breton (Celtic) *lai* in particular. Indeed, Stuart Sperry hears—probably quite accurately—echoes of Celtic lore in "La Belle Dame," for which Keats's possession of *Celtic Researches* might well have tuned the poet's ear.[26]

While the bulk of the evidence rests with the three odes to be examined below ("Ode to Psyche," "Ode to a Nightingale," and "Ode on a Grecian Urn"), two lesser-known poems require attention as possible literary descendents of Marie's poetry: "Sleep and Poetry" (1816) and the "Epistle to J. H. Reynolds" (1819). Themes and images attributable to Marie's *Guigemar*—available to Keats in Wells's second volume of *Fabliaux and Tales*—abound. The Breton tale's plot is propelled forward literally and metaphorically when a prince scornful of love but wounded by one of its arrows boards a magical ship and collapses into a deep sleep. The otherwise unmanned vessel transports him almost to the very door of a castle in which a beautiful young woman—the victim of a jealous, elderly husband—languishes in a locked room. The two meet, and the story takes its natural course, albeit with a good many unforeseeable twists of fate. Sleep's bounty for Keats in "Sleep and Poetry"—"what there may be worthy in these rhymes / I partly owe to him" (and to the voyage of imagination taken on his friend's couch) (349-50)—echoes other scenes in which rest is productive of good, perhaps Milton's nightly inspiration by the muse in *Paradise Lost* and Adam's Eve-creating slumber, but also, perhaps, Prince Guigemar's profound, death-like sleep aboard the fairy-ship that brings him to his lady-love. Sleep, then, is no less effective as a vehicle for literary production in Keats's poem than in Marie's *lai*. Further, the ship itself is one of the most richly delineated images in all of Marie's *Lais*, with its "silken sails / Just bellying, [that] caught gently the rising gales" and "its ebon sides [that] shot dazzling sheen / Of silvery rays with mingled gold between."[27] A surprisingly similar vessel, ostensibly remembered from a painting by Claude entitled *The Enchanted Castle* but bearing little resemblance to the unremarkable boat represented there, drifts into the reader's ken in Keats's "Epistle to Reynolds." Keats's ship lacks the "ebon sides" of Marie's creation but is succinctly denoted to be "a golden galley with silken trim!" (56). Like Marie's supernaturally-driven boat, this one, though a galley, seems to be impelled by some unseen force, for no oarsmen are mentioned—only "three rows of oars…lightening moment-whiles / Into the verdurous bosom of those isles" and "toward the shade under the castle wall" (59-60). Guigemar's frigate similarly approaches not a bay but the very castle itself, as the lady's jealous husband has taken care that no easy entrance by land is available. It seems, then, that if indeed Keats looked to Marie for inspiration, it was not necessarily a mere whim of his later career; he might have done so as early as 1816—the year of "Sleep and Poetry's" composition and three years before he penned the odes.

"Ode to Psyche," usually considered one of the earliest of the 1819 odes, is overtly pseudo-classical in its matter and imagery, but its diction and final image draw the poem irresistibly toward romance; Marie's presiding figure may be discerned, however faintly. To begin with, Keats himself averred in an April 1819 letter that the ode was "the first and only one [of the recent compositions copied into the epistle] with which I have taken even moderate pains" (II.105-06); if this is so, he would logically have had more leisure to mull over various mental "distillations" of his readings.[28] Thus, one of what are generally considered Keats's least allusive poems (the odes) might well be seen in a different guise. More importantly, as Bate notices in "La Belle Dame," there is a "clean simplicity and brevity" of diction[29] at certain points that may be attributable if not to Marie, at least to another poet of her ilk. Though Bate suggests that this simplicity was typically associated by Romantics with all literature of the Middle Ages, such a mindset does not seem to apply to other medievalistic Keatsian productions of the same year, like *The Eve of St. Agnes,* whose prolixity constitutes one of its chief beauties. As Jan Nelson makes clear, simplicity, or, to use the proper rhetorical term, abbreviation, was not the norm among medieval writers; rather, most were prone to amplification.[30]

So Marie was indeed unique, and her tendency to abbreviate could have only been intensified by Le Grand's, Way's, and Ellis's abridgements and abstracts of her work.

The brevity of "Ode to Psyche" is not a particularly consistent feature but rather a function of various compressed word formations that may be said to be adjectival adaptations of even older Anglo-Saxon kennings: "'Mid hush'd, cool-rooted flowers, fragrant-eyed, / Blue, silver-white, and budded Tyrian, / They lay calm-breathing on the bedded grass" (13-15). It seems that the compression of plot and description in Marie's tales is here appropriated for a lush and densely-conceived image.

The possible influence of the *Lais* is more readily apparent in the introduction of an image that appears in at least two other Keats poems (the "Epistle to Reynolds" and "Ode to a Nightingale"): the magic casement.[31] Two of Marie's twelve *Lais,* namely *Yonec* and *Laüstic,* employ windows both realistically and fantastically as indispensable images and plot elements. The latter tale will be discussed later with reference to the Nightingale ode, but the casement in *Yonec*—which admits the hawk-turned-human lover to the imprisoned young wife's chamber— resembles the description of the mental shrine Keats intends to prepare for the newly-deified Psyche, with its "casement ope at night / To let the warm Love in!" (66-67). In both poems, the woman/goddess is confined—in Marie's, by a jealous old husband, and in Keats's by the poet himself—yet in each there is access for a supernatural lover, whether he be a hawk-man or Cupid himself. To be sure, lovers have been leaping through windows and into the beds of willing maidens since the beginning of mythic time; yet the juxtaposition of a realistic and commonplace architectural feature with elements that are both supernatural in form and quite as natural as love itself is a touch in every way worthy of Marie.

"Ode to a Nightingale" conjures for the well-versed reader a multiplicity of texts to which the poem might implicitly allude. Helen Vendler argues for the intertextual nature of the ode even in the case of stanza 5 ("I cannot see the flowers at my feet, / But in embalmed darkness guess each sweet"), which at first glance seems the least allusive of the stanzas.[32] Aside from the ubiquity of the bird in many literatures as a symbol of love and often-attendant death, several of Keats's other poems, even as early as an 1815 verse epistle, bid the reader listen to the song of the nightingale, as Thomas Shippey does in his excellent article on the subject.[33] In that early lyric, nightingales in "covert branches...have always sung / In leafy quiet" (45-47)—an image which seems to anticipate the "melodious plot of beechen green" in the Nightingale ode. The "Epistle to Reynolds," so rife with imagery of all kinds, ironically asserts that imagination "spoils the singing of the nightingale" (85), and in the sonnet "Bards of passion," the bird "doth sing / Not a senseless, trancéd thing, / But divine melodious truth" (17-20). However, none of these philomelic versions seem quite like the one in the ode. Besides, such incestuous references—never striking out beyond Keats's own corpus of poetry—might lead to increasingly closed-minded interpretations.

The two generally acknowledged sources for the Nightingale ode outside Keats's own work are Dryden's translation of a pseudo-Chaucerian poem entitled "The Flower and the Leaf" and Coleridge's "The Nightingale." In the case of the former, the similarities are confined primarily to setting[34]; in the latter instance, there is little similarity at all, though both Keats's and Coleridge's poems ostensibly "follow Coleridge's [own] injunction that he [the poet] should refuse to be carried away from natural perception by the inherited mythological legend of Philomela's sorrow."[35] Keats did not seem especially to reverence Coleridge; they met only once by coincidence, and the young poet wryly recounted the older one's ramblings thus: "In those two Miles he broached a thousand things—let me see if I can give you a list—Nightingales, Poetry—on Poetical sensation—Metaphysics—Different genera and species of Dreams—Nightmare"—and the catalogue goes on (II.88-89). While the poets' interests are remarkably similar, Keats certainly "does not entirely follow Coleridge," as Vendler points out.[36] Indeed, the last notes heard by the poet are described as part of a "plaintive anthem" worthy of the unfortunate Philomela herself (75). To what, then, does the poem owe its unforgettable use of an otherwise outworn symbol? Whence came that music, both hauntingly real and palpably enchanting?

To say that Keats's mind was capable of producing a poem without harkening to medieval echoes is, of course, entirely reasonable. Even so, the fact that it is already commonly associated with a medieval text ("The Flower and the Leaf"), as well as the reference to the magic casements, might just as reasonably point the reader backward in time to Marie's *Laüstic*. At least one critic sees in those casements not merely a repetition of the ones in the "Epistle to Reynolds" but an image borrowed from Celtic lore;[37] this observation in turn suggests a possible debt to a Breton *lai*.

The particular *lai* in question—*Laüstic*—presents yet another unhappily wedded wife whose husband's castle so nearly adjoins that of her admirer that the two may easily toss love-tokens back and forth and gaze longingly at each other whenever passion prompts them. The lady is restless at night and often visits the window; her husband becomes suspicious, and she claims that her insomnia is induced by her love of the nightingale's song. Probably well aware of the amorous implications of such an excuse—as Shippey convincingly argues[38]—the husband captures the bird, wrings its neck, and, in a fit of jealous rage, hurls it at his wife. She conveys the message of her husband's discovery to her lover by embroidering the incident on a winding sheet for the bird, and the unfortunate knightly lover seals the nightingale's corpse in a reliquary that he keeps with him always.

Thematically, each poem appears to be the inverse of the other. Marie's narrative presents the sense of sight as the only trustworthy means of communication, while Keats's lyric distrusts vision and depends almost entirely on what can be perceived aurally—"for here there is no light" (38). When vision is exchanged for hearing in the *lai*—when the wife disingenuously declares that she is roused each night by the nightingale's song—disaster ensues that can only be communicated to her lover by visual signs embroidered on the nightingale's diminutive winding-sheet. When the poet's attention shifts from the heard to the seen—when he begins to ask himself whether his reverie was "a vision or a waking dream," (79)—the nightingale falls silent. Thus, silence is a key point of intersection for the medieval and Romantic poems: in the one, it immortalizes a love that is otherwise dead by preserving it in the jeweled casket thereafter worn by the knightly lover; in the other, it deadens imagination and provokes the poet's self-questioning final line: "Do I wake or sleep?" (80). Consciousness is itself a crucial issue in both texts, but again the situations are reversed. Only when wakeful at night can the lovers of *Laüstic* dally with each other in their odd, insubstantial way, while only in a half-sleep can the poet sense and create. Further, fancy in the *lai* (or rather the wife's inventive excuse for staying up nights) cheats her all too well; her imagination quite literally spoils the singing of the nightingale. In the ode, the poet complains of the "deceiving elf" whose powers prove to be all too impotent. Of course, the chief thematic elements in *Laüstic,* as in many a muséd rhyme, are Love and Death, and the one precedes the other in quite the usual way, even if Death literally touches only the hapless bird. In the Nightingale ode the same thematic pair appears, but Death has curiously turned lover.

What is perhaps most surprising in the juxtaposition of these texts is the subtle reversal of typical generic expectations. Marie's *Laüstic* is remarkably free from enchantment, even if one takes into consideration her idiosyncratic realization of the romance as a form. Even its casements are mere windows and nothing more. By way of another ironic reversal, Keats's ode, despite its dignified tone, is more typically Marie-like in its fantastic jumble of real and unreal (cf. *Yonec*) than is the *lai* in question.

Perhaps comparison by way of point-for-point contrast is too unorthodox a method for establishing intertextuality; if so, it may be easily exchanged for another approach. Ellis assures his readers, oddly enough, that "the adventure it [*Laüstic*] relates is as insipid as possible"; perhaps he did not translate it well enough to appreciate anything beyond what he patronizingly terms its "picturesque descriptions" (of which there are few).[39] But if he had had the as yet unwritten Nightingale ode and a truer translation of Marie's text before him, he could not have failed to notice a most peculiar similarity. In a very brief summary from the French, Donovan underscores a line that might well have, in either the original or eighteenth-century French, immersed itself in the catalytic depths of Keats's mind to emerge unforgettably in the first stanza of the ode: "Nights when her [the female lover's] testy husband asks why she is getting up and where she is going, she replies that *whoever fails to hear the nightingale enjoys none of the world's pleasure*" (my italics).[40] Witness this sentiment more lyrically rendered in fine Keatsian form as the poet defends his melancholy mood: " 'Tis not through envy of thy happy lot / But being too happy in thine happiness" (5-6). Serendipitously, the *Lais* had just been republished in French in 1819, and Keats was fluent in the language.

Hence it is clear that in both texts emotional realism is of utmost importance—and that, implicitly, emotion is reified in either the body or the song of the nightingale. That is, the bird serves as a striking objective correlative in both Marie's *lai* and Keats's ode.[41] In *Laüstic*, the connection is so apparent as to be almost archetypal, and yet it is not at all static and is to some degree ambivalent. The bird's singing, though entirely distinct from the lovers' wholly voyeuristic love affair, symbolizes their mutual pleasure. Yet it is at the moment of the wife's attempted dissimulation that their unconsummated joy in the sight of each other is doomed. The reader is reminded of Keats's disappointment in "Beauty [that] cannot keep her lustrous eyes" and "new Love [that cannot] pine at them beyond tomorrow" (29-30). Further, the bird's corpse is literally written over with the tale of the lovers' sorrow. At rest in its tiny reliquary, the nightingale embodies the lover's undying remembrance of their love—and it is thus in one sense comparable to Keats's "Immortal Bird."

One might say that the Keatsian nightingale resists its traditional objective correlative function, but that it does so eventually in vain. Almost bereft of all sense, pained by "a drowsy numbness," the poet is nearly incapable of feeling at all and desperately imposes on the "winged Dryad" the opposite of his dulled but still aching consciousness. While he mourns decay and untimely death, the nightingale "singest of summer in full-throated ease" (10); while the illumination and inspiration of the Queen-moon cheers the bird, the poet is trapped where there is no light. Yet the poet is at last tolled "back from thee to my sole self" (72), so that he—much like the unfortunate lovers—can no longer experience even vicariously the happiness he attributed to the bird. Worse yet, the nightingale itself seems finally to partake of the poet's true emotions and not what he wishes them to be, for its "*plaintive* anthem fades" (75, my italics) but fails to wing away the "drowsy numbness."

What may strengthen the notion of *Laüstic* as a Keatsian source is its otherwise uncanny anticipation not just of the Nightingale ode but also of the poem usually read as its companion-piece—"Ode on a Grecian Urn." The final image in Marie's *lai* is of the bird sealed and silent in its reliquary: it conflates the central figures of the two odes so that they merge into one meaningful *objet d'art*. It was for Keats's poetic genius, nearly seven hundred years later, to resurrect the bird and discourse upon the urn.

"Things cannot to the will / Be settled, but they tease us out of thought," writes a twenty-two-year-old Keats to Reynolds in 1817 (I.181). So it is, not only with the Urn, then as yet not written into existence, but also with any study of Keats's sources. In the end, "a little speculation" may have to content the scholar as it did—perhaps—the poet. Yet the very impulse toward source study reveals Keats to be as much an un-Romantic Romantic as a supposedly unpoetical poet. Despite the Romantic obsession with authenticity, Keats continually applied his artistic distillery as wholeheartedly as any medieval man or woman of letters. Likewise, Marie's anachronistically humanistic perspective[42]—the proto-modernism of her sympathy for human frailty—renders facile assumptions of quaint archaism woefully inadequate. Considering Keats's fitfully ambivalent attitude toward human power and artistic vision—the twin terrors that he might "cease to be / Before my pen has gleaned my teeming brain" of its store of "high romance" ("When I have fears" 1-2, 6) and that, after all, "fancy cannot cheat so well / As she is fam'd to do" ("Nightingale" 73-74)— the quintessential Romantic might well harbor more overtly medieval sentiments than the twelfth-century Gallic bard. The chameleon poet, contrary to nature, does not merely disappear into the fabric of a medieval text but summarily robs it of its somber dye.

*TUFTS UNIVERSITY*

NOTES

[1] J. Caitlin Finlayson, "Medieval Sources for Keatsian Creation in *La Belle Dame Sans Merci*," *Philological Quarterly* 79 (2002): 225-47 (225). Finlayson's fine source study for Keats's "La Belle Dame sans Merci" deploys both external and textual evidence to support the theory that Keats's "La Belle Dame" is not primarily a Spenserian text. Citing the pseudo-Chaucerian *La Belle Dame sans Mercy* that appears in Keats's 1782 edition of Chaucer, Finlayson argues for its influence on the Keats ballad.

[2] Hyder Edward Rollins, ed., *The Letters of John Keats*, (Cambridge, Mass.: Harvard UP, 1958). Hereafter, the volume and page numbers will appear in parentheses within the text. In an October 1818 epistle to Richard Woodhouse, Keats defines himself and his poetic philosophy thus: "As to the poetical Character itself (I mean the sort of which, if I am any thing, I am a member; that sort distinguished from the [W]ordsworthian or egotistical sublime; which is a thing per se and stands alone) it is not itself—it has no self—it is every thing [sic]and nothing....It has as much delight in conceiving an Iago as an Imogen. What shocks the virtuous philosopher, delights the camelion Poet....A Poet

is the most unpoetical of any thing in existence; because he has no Identity—he is continually in for—and filling some other Body—the Sun, the Moon, the Sea and Men and Women who are creatures of impulse are poetical and have about them an unchangeable attribute—the poet has none; no identity—he is certainly the most unpoetical of God's Creatures" (I.386-87).

[3] Glyn S. Burgess and Keith Busby, eds. and trans., *The Lais of Marie de France* (London: Penguin, 1999), 9.

[4] Burgess and Busby, 41. In the "Prologue" to her *Lais,* Marie argues that "it was customary for the ancients, in the books which they wrote (Priscian testifies to this), to express themselves very obscurely so that those in later generations, who had to learn them, could provide a gloss for the text and put the finishing touches to their meaning": why should she not, then, do much the same thing and more for the *lais* when she "made poems from them"?

[5] Frank L. Owings, *The Keats Library: A Descriptive Catalogue* (London: Keats-Shelley Memorial Association, 1978), ix.

[6] Sidney Colvin, *John Keats: His Life and Poetry, His Friends, Critics, and After-Fame* (New York: Scribner, 1917), 557. Woodhouse's catalogue does not specify the book's publisher, but one may reasonably assume that it was Taylor and Hessey.

[7] Amy Lowell, *John Keats* (Cambridge, Mass.: Riverside, 1925), 426.

[8] Colvin, 88-89.

[9] Lowell, 426.

[10] Colvin, 175.

[11] Colvin, 175, 186.

[12] Robert Gittings, *John Keats* (Boston: Little, Brown, 1968), 277.

[13] Colvin, 33.

[14] George Ellis, *Specimens of Early English Metrical Romances* (New York: AMS, 1968), 46.

[15] John Keats, *Complete Poems,* ed. Jack Stillinger (Cambridge, Mass.: Belknap, 1982). This and all further Keatsian poetic references are made by line number only and are taken from this edition.

[16] Walter Jackson Bate, *John Keats* (Cambridge, Mass.: Belknap, 1963), 315.

[17] Morris Dickstein, *Keats and His Poetry: A Study in Development* (Chicago and London: University of Chicago Press, 1969), 191.

[18] Donald Sands, Introduction, *Middle English Verse Romances* (New York: Holt, Rinehart, and Winston, 1966), 1-11 (4).

[19] Paula Clifford, *Marie de France: Lais,* Critical Guides to French Texts 16 (London: Grant & Cutler, 1982). Clifford's article discusses *Yonec* and others of the tales in which "supernatural elements are transformed into human, Christian ones" (61). Clifford further argues that "in *Laüstic* and *Chevrefoil* the tragic note is complimented by a particularly realistic treatment of emotions" (76).

[20] Martin Donovan, *The Breton Lay: A Guide to Varieties* (Notre Dame: University of Notre Dame Press, 1969), 33.

[21] Jack Stillinger, "Keats and Romance," *Studies in English Literature* 8 (1968): 593-605 (595).

[22] Bate, 284.

[23] Keats was fond of setting for himself hyperbolic goals; it is sometimes difficult to

determine whether he did so in jest or in earnest. After completing the fourth act of *Otho the Great* in August 1819, he wrote to Benjamin Bailey thus: "It was the opinion of my friends that I should never be able to write a scene—I will endeavour to wipe away the prejudice....One of my Ambitions is to make as great a revolution in modern dramatic writing as Kean has done in acting." Yet he immediately undercuts his statement by linking it with his desire to "upset the drawling of the bluestocking literary world" and by imagining his friends "drink[ing] a dozen of Claret on my tomb" in a grotesque posthumous celebration of his "successes" (I.139). Three months later he dreams of "writing...a few fine Plays—my greatest ambition—when I do feel ambitious" (II.234). Keats is forever tantalizing his readers with his intentions and simultaneously befuddling them.

[24] Robert Gitttings, *The Mask of Keats: A Study of Problems* (Cambridge, Mass.: Harvard University Press, 1956), 74. Gittings identifies this phrase—once apparently thought to be a mere Chattertonian effusion—as a reference to a genuine medieval source.

[25] Andrew Motion, *Keats* (New York: Ferrar, Straus, and Giroux, 1997), 449; Burgess and Busby, 17, 26. A dilemma arises if a literal equation is made between Marie's *Lais* and the productions of medieval southern France. The poetry of the Provençal troubadours was not exactly the same as that of the northern trouvÈres, and the Breton *lais* technically belong in neither category. This seeming obstacle to any Keatsian allusion to Marie's work evaporates, though, when one realizes that even though the Provençal genre developed separately, it migrated north in the middle of the twelfth century—just before the twenty-year period which supposedly saw the composition of Marie's *Lais* (1170-1190) (Burgess and Busby, 17). Further, the Breton *lai* could be posited as "a transitional genre between earlier Provençal love lyrics and the romance" (Burgess and Busby, 26). It is doubtful, however, that Keats would have cared much for such fastidious delineations of genre.

[26] Stuart Sperry, *Keats the Poet* (Princeton: Princeton University Press, 1973), 235.

[27] Pierre Le Grand D'Assey, *Fabliaux or Tales, Abridged from French Manuscripts of the XIIth and XIIIth Centuries*, trans. G.L. Way (London, 1796), 5.

[28] Bate, 478.

[29] Bate, 478.

[30] Jan Nelson, "Abbreviated Style in *Les Lais de Marie de France*," *Romance Quarterly* 39 (1992): 131-43 (132-33).

[31] M. R. Ridley, *Keats's Craftsmanship: A Study in Poetic Development* (Lincoln: University of Nebraska Press, 1963), 227. Of course, the persistence of this imagery may be merely the effect of an unaccounted-for authorial preference; Ridley confidently asserts that "Keats had all his life a love for windows"—but as Keats's letters do not abound with literal or metaphorical window references, another explanation might be appropriate.

[32] Helen Vendler, *The Odes of John Keats* (Cambridge, Mass.: Belknap, 1983), 84-85.

[33] Thomas A. Shippey, "Listening to the Nightingale," *Comparative Literature* 22 (1970): 46-60. Shippey's article particularly discusses *Laüstic* in connection with Bernart de Ventadorn's *The Owl and the Nightingale*.

[34] For further discussion of the two poems, see Gittings's *John Keats* (316-17).

[35] Vendler, 31.

[36] Vendler, 82.

[37] Lowell, 247-48.

[38] Shippey explains that "listening to the nightingale" had symbolic meaning beyond the usual associations of the bird with love's loss; the husband would have understood the illicit amorous subtext of his lady's alibi (51-52).
[39] Ellis, 58.
[40] Donovan, 30.
[41] In *The Anonymous Marie de France* (Chicago and London: U of Chicago P, 2003), R. Howard Bloch identifies the nightingale's reliquary as an objective correlative for the *lai* itself but does not discuss the bird's function as an objective correlative for the lovers' emotional states.
[42] See R. W. Southern's *Medieval Humanism and Other Studies* (New York and Evanston: Harper and Row, 1970) for a clear-eyed study of what he terms "medieval humanism" in the period between 1100 and 1320, "one of the greatest ages of humanism in the history of Europe: perhaps the greatest of all" (31).

# Tolkien, Ricoeur, and Eliot:
## The World of the Text and the 20th-Century Wasteland

### Edward L. Risden

In a brief headnote to the Ballantine edition of the *Lord of the Rings* (1965 edition), Peter Beagle intuits that "in the end it is Middle-earth and its dwellers that we love, not Tolkien's considerable gifts in showing it to us," for "the world he charts was there long before him" as part of "our most common nightmares, daydreams, and twilight fantasies." Beagle adds, "he found them a place to live, a green alternative to each day's madness here in a poisoned world"; Beagle saw, I think, the key to Tolkien's fictional accomplishment and his success in realizing it, the key perhaps to all fantasy, if not all fiction: Middle-earth appears before us as a world we already know and, despite its dangers, love. Somewhere between the printed product of Tolkien's imagination and the active, organic, semi-responsive world of our own, we meet in a compelling place, as Beagle suggests, of our mutual construction, or as Tolkien might say, of our sub-creation. Who among us wouldn't wish, at least for a short time, to visit that world?

I would like to suggest here that we desire that world not just for the pleasure it provides us, but also for what it lets, or makes, us do: we enter Tolkien's "greenworld" to learn something about how to deal with evil, so that we might return better prepared to deal with our own "wasteland" or to create a better alternative to it. Like Eliot, Tolkien implies an apocalyptic present, but one more like that of the later Eliot, though sadder: we may not be too late to recover something of the greenworld, though we probably lack the fortitude to do it, and so must subsist on the memory and fantasy alone.

Some useful theoretical background comes from two essays by Paul Ricoeur. In one, a response to Northrop Frye's *Anatomy of Criticism*, I find a particularly helpful recurring motif, the idea that between the author's product, the text, and ourselves as imaginative respondents moves a multi-dimensional "world of the text":

> I see Frye's second phase [in his theory of symbols] as the nexus or turning-point between suspended reference and recreated reference, what I would call, in a vocabulary close to Hans-Georg Gadamer's, reference to the world of the text. To the extent that the poem unfolds in some hypothetical dimension, it also projects a world that we might inhabit. (8)

That is, the world of the text makes no special claim to "reality," nor does it detach itself from reality; one could say, though, that it acquires an especially useful kind of applicability as a connection between a potentially instructive symbolic system and the daily life in which we often need, despite modern reluctance to admit it, instruction. And a symbol, or a text, or a world, may simultaneously attract and repulse:

> [T]his polar structure is itself unified by the strength of the desire that configures both the infinitely desirable and its contrary, the infinitely detestable....[A]ll imagery is inadequate in relation to the apocalyptic imagery of fulfillment and yet at the same time in search of it. (10)[1]

Any "real" world must have, according to anyone's taste, positive and negative attributes, and because any real world must come to an end, its inhabitants may prophesy and prepare: we can learn how they do that and how we may do that.

In a second essay, this one on the process of interpreting narrative, Ricoeur, emerging from a background of Monroe Beardsley's work, writes,

> I assume that it is the task of an hermeneutic to disentangle from the referential claims of any literary work the kind of world it displays....[W]hat is to be interpreted in a text is a proposed world that I might inhabit and wherein I might project my own most possibilities [sic]. (149)[2]

Essentially, then, all literature aims at something "fantastic," the creation of a shared world of mutual becoming. Why do serious readers project themselves into texts, for pleasure only or because they search for something that makes sense, as Tolkien and his generation tried to shape a battleground that their readers could tolerate as they, the writers, struggled to make sense of what they'd unforgettably learned? Essentially readers, as do writers, look for, in Eliot's term, the objective correlative: the image not of the original thing itself, but the one that evokes the emotions of the original in the way an audience can best understand and share.

When we write, we parallel, one may say, William Blake's alter ego *Los*: we must create our own system or be enslaved by someone else's; when we read, we parallel Blake as visionary: allowing ourselves to inhabit the envisioned world, we return then to hammer out its application in the "mental fight" of the present grimy, political world. The visionary world may appear to exhibit a greater or lesser degree of verisimilitude, but regardless it serves as the necessary ground of adventure, and the quality of the adventure determines what we may experience and learn and what boon we may bring home. Clearly, generations of readers have returned from Tolkien with a boon, since we continue to read, rewrite, and film his stories.

Of course, part of what attracts us to Middle-earth derives from Tolkien's array of characters: who wouldn't happily meet elves strolling on a cool, starlit fall evening or Tom Bombadil marching in his yellow boots, protecting woods that we love? Hobbits, ents, dwarves emerge as allies with the special powers we desire, and even the evil characters, orcs, oversized spiders, wizards gone bad, look little worse than our modern street criminals, terrorists, news conglomerates, and politicians and the weapons they readily wield against us. Part comes also from his geography: many a broken-Moria day the gray havens look awfully inviting, however hard they may be to find. Part comes from the traditional monomythic elements of the plot, but also from the fact that in following Bilbo and Frodo, we depart from the powerful hero to the everyday mortal of more modest means. Most of us relate better to Bilbo, Frodo, and Sam than to Gandalf, Aragorn, and Arwen: in them we find the joy of life, but also its inescapable mortality.

As Tom Shippey argues in much of his critical work on Tolkien,[3] Tolkien wrote not as an escape from our quotidian world, but as a way of moving into a realm where he could explore and grapple with the problem of evil—I would say as a response not only to World War I, but also to the devolving sense of the Twentieth Century as Wasteland. Tolkien's world grew, as many critics have commented, from a combination of philology and a desire to create for Britain its own mythology, free of Mediterranean oppression. Its rationale, geography, and inhabitants take full shape in the

*Silmarillion*, but its human heart fully emerges only in the *Lord of the Rings*, even more so than in *The Hobbit*. Bilbo's story, gloriously fun in its adventurous topography, allows for evil, even for its ability to hold sway in the world, but it postpones the necessary consequences in human action that must result from evil's persistence. Smaug functions "apocalyptically" locally, but not generally; with the defeat of Sauron and the consequences thereof—including the destruction of the ring—comes the end of an age. Only in the story of the destruction of the One Ring amidst a crumbling world do we bury the dead, retake, for a time, the greenwood, and exchange our spindly *shantih* for the smithy that the modern world has demanded we build: we learn that with making comes the potential to un-make, for ill or for good.

As Shippey argues, Tolkien—and his whole generation—met convulsions that neither the wisdom of the ancients nor current authorities could explain: the devastation of modern warfare and the addictive nature of evil ("Post-War" 233, 228); what no one could accomplish through "realism," Tolkien's generation sought to explain through fantasy. Good fantasy works not because it provides an escape from our "real world," but because it creates an alternative world in which we as readers and critics can attend at least the confrontation if not the solution to the "great problems," neither finding ourselves excluded by politics nor dying in the process of fighting them. By sharing them, we can work through them with the characters in a world we believe worthy of saving and, we hope, carry over something of those solutions to quotidian life. The secret, I suppose, is that one must love both worlds and find them worth saving. As Shippey shows in *J.R.R. Tolkien: Author of the* Century, Tolkien's creation of a whole world, full of maps, languages, and peculiar local customs, beyond the adventures in which we share through all its significant history (69, 68), teaches us "'what it would be like' to be there" (6)—not just in Middle-earth, but also in the trenches of World War I or in the midst of a council of the Mighty as they seek not to ignore or profit from our problems, but to solve them. We depart our wasteland, not merely for another like it, but more for the Hildegardian *veriditas* of the Last Homely House and the quest that issues from it, where we learn, perhaps, how to bring the greening home and apply it locally and subcutaneously.

Here Eliot formally enters my critical narrative. *The Waste Land*, which first appeared in 1921, deals, of course, with both the external and internal traumas of World War I. The first of its five sections, "The Burial of the Dead," seems an obvious, necessary, detached, ritualistic response to the end of the war: before we do anything else, we must bury the dead. The second section, "A Game of Chess," buries seduction beneath equally detached intellectual intensity. Part three, "The Fire Sermon," unveils a rape beneath the Buddha's famous call to release ourselves from the passions of the senses. The very brief fourth section, "Death by Water," carries additional, barely noted, pointless death rather than the baptism that might provide necessary renewal. The concluding section, "What the Thunder Said," rather than looking back to what survivors might have seen as an "apocalyptic" war, prophesies instead *another* apocalypse to come: not even in his own notes does Eliot cite his true source, which comes from the Bible's Book of Revelation, Chapter 10.

In John's Apocalypse, after the opening of the seventh seal comes a silence of half an hour, then seven angels appear, and the first six sound their trumpets. The seventh angel descends from Heaven with a little book in his hands; he places his right foot on the sea and his left on the land, then thunders forth like a lion. John, about to write what the angel speaks, hears a voice from Heaven say, "Seal up the things which the seven peals of thunder have spoken, and do not write them." John then eats the little book and must go forth among the nations to prophesy. While Eliot looks away from the history of Europe and the "unreal city" of the postwar West toward the dubious mysticism of the East, in the background we may hear the pseudo-Johanine voice speaking exactly what, after the first war, we don't need to hear: we thought we'd seen the "war to end all wars," but we hadn't seen anything yet. In fact, the wasteland hardly had time to heal before war would assault it once more, by land and sea alike.

Tolkien (more in the *Lord of the Rings* than elsewhere) responded, I think, to his own vision of the between-wars wasteland with a creation, his Middle-earth, less cryptic than Eliot's, and with a greater willingness to live in the present and to hope despite what loomed potentially as a hopeless future.[4] Think of the Shire, Rivendell, Lothlorien: they resist Mordor and its growing wastelands. Think of Gandalf, Elrond, Galadriel, and the Fellowship: they resist Sauron, Saruman, and Ringwraiths. Most importantly, unlike Boromir, the hobbits together resist the desire to use the Ring, and they do have luck on their side. As Shippey points out ("Post-War" 228), the potential for the greatest evil of all occurs when, within Mount Doom, Frodo nearly fails to destroy the Ring: without Sam and, most ironically, Gollum, he probably would have failed, as might any of us in such a circumstance: the apocalyptic moment, Tolkien might have said, comes for all, even the smallest of us, and tests each one.

For those readers who have seen the film version of *The Fellowship of the Ring*, recall Peter Jackson's visions of the clashing armies when Isildur struck the Ring from Sauron's finger; Frodo, supine before the Ringwraiths on Weathertop; the dead Moria, with its Balrog rising from unimaginable depths; or Saruman's Orc-pits beneath Orthanc: hell appears in many forms, but none so terrifying, finally, as the wasteland within, when in *The Return of the King* the small hero's will to goodness, duty, and sacrifice nearly fail. Like the Old English heroic verse that formed the centerpiece of much of Tolkien's study, the thematic, ethical center of *LOTR* emerges quietly as steadfast courage, blithe persistence in one's code of conduct, belief in the glory one wins through laudable behavior, and willingness to sacrifice personal gain to share peace.

For Tolkien, fighting evil means resisting the wasteland on both fronts, internally as well as externally, even if that effort requires leaving one's own bucolic haven. The "world of his text" provides the ground where we may thoroughly experience the love of that green peace, yet come to understand that for love of it we may lose some of it in hopes saving its essence. A similar theme arises, for fans of Japanese animation, in the film *Princess Mononoke*: growing into one's responsibilities means preserving what we can and recovering what we must of what's green and good. Because we may identify evil, we can also learn to identify good and aim to maintain it. We may fail, and we may succeed; a "fantasy" author aims to create a world in which we can tell the difference and from which we may take something to apply in our own world, for its betterment and ours. As a Christian writer who created a non- or pre-Christian world, Tolkien allowed his creation to remain free of dogma, but not of moral or ethical imperatives. Perhaps even in our relativistic times, we don't shy from confronting those imperatives as much as we expect we would; perhaps fantasy allows us to confront what politics obscures in our own world. Apocalypse lies beyond the wasteland, and we have yet to reach it together.

Finally, Tolkien's world shares with ours violence, horror, suffering, perversion, weakness, death; it also shares with ours kindness, self-sacrifice, courage, and the love of things that grow, companionship, a good meal.[5] We inhabit his world with only the briefest hesitation—and most of us who have entered once re-enter it often—because there courage and goodness can win, if they have a bit of luck. Whether that fact represents, in the long run, fantasy or truth remains for us to prove, but most of us, I think, wish to live in a world that has at least that much potential. Of that potential our best fiction, Tolkien knew, aims to convince us.

*ST. NORBERT COLLEGE*

NOTES

[1] "'Anatomy of Criticism' or the Order of Paradigms," in *Center and Labyrinth: Essays in Honor of Northrop Frye*. Ed. Eleanor Cook at al. (Toronto: U of Toronto P, 1983), 1-12.

[2] "Narrative and Hermeneutics," in *Essays on Aesthetics: Perspectives on the Work of Monroe C. Beardsley*, ed. John Fisher. (Philadelphia: Temple UP, 1983), 149ff.

[3] See particularly "Tolkien as a Post-War Writer'" in *Scholarship and Fantasy: Proceedings of The Tolkien Phenomenon*, ed. K. J. Battarbee. (Turku, Finland: 1993), pages 217-36, and more recently *J. R. R. Tolkien: Author of the Century*, (Boston: Houghton Mifflin, 2000).

[4] Tolkien mentions Eliot only twice in his letters, in both cases briefly. In letter 261 he writes of C. S. Lewis, "That his [Lewis's] literary opinions were ever dictated by envy (as in the case of T. S. Eliot) is a grotesque calumny. After all it is possible to dislike Eliot with some intensity even if one has no aspirations to poetic laurels oneself." In letter 266, after noting the demise of his former tutor, C. T. Onions, he mentions Eliot's death and adds a note of distaste with respect to John Masefield's verse on Eliot published in *The Times*. See Humphrey Carpenter's edition (with Christopher Tolkien) of *The Letters of J. R. R. Tolkien*, (Boston: Houghton Mifflin, 1981), pages 350 and 353. These passages suggest that Tolkien had no great admiration for Eliot or his work.

[5] Part of the appeal of Middle-earth comes of course from its enormous complexity, from Tolkien's effort to create a fully realized world. As Jonathan Evans has pointed out, Tolkien's "capacity for decentering the anthropological perspective" allows for some stunning effects both narratival and emotional ("The Anthropology of Arda," in *Tolkien the Medievalist*, ed. Jane Chance, London and New York: Routledge, 2003, page 197). Gergely Nagy argues the significance of the "impression of depth" of the world that Tolkien creates by "mythopoeic" means, by creating a nexus of tales that allows him or his readers to "assign equal importance to *all texts* in the corpus and their interrelations" ("The Great Chain of Reading: (Inter-)textual relations and the Technique of Mythopoesis in the Turin Story," also in Chance's volume, pages 239 and 253). That is, allusions with stories behind them and stories behind *them* fan out into a world with its own complete history far beyond even the vast landscape we see. Complexity gives the world a greater capability to suggest "reality."

# The Power of his Horror:
## Abjection and Macbeth

James R. Keller

This essay is devoted to the scrutiny of a single issue surrounding the critical reception of Shakespeare's *Macbeth*: the potential disunity of the titular character. When the captain describes Macbeth's heroism to Duncan at the beginning of the play, the audience encounters an individual who, on the battlefield, is willing to "bathe in reeking wounds," to "memorize another Golgotha" (I.i.39-40),[1] and to "unseam" a rebel leader "from the nave to the chops" (I.i.22), actions which suggest a battle-hardened nature that does not recoil from savage violence; however, in Act II, he is so horrified by the blood of King Duncan that he is unable to save himself from detection and must rely upon the remorseless resolution of his wife. The man whose sword "smoked with bloody execution" (I.i.18) dares not look upon Duncan's slaughtered body. Since it is not credible that Macbeth is merely squeamish about blood, and it is still less credible that Shakespeare was unconcerned about the unity of the central character in one of his late tragedies, Macbeth's horror and revulsion toward Duncan's murder must have a rational explanation.

Shakespearean scholars have approached Macbeth's emotional caprices in the same way that they have attempted to solve the paradoxes that abound within the play, proceeding upon the assumption that the disparate traits in Macbeth's nature will evaporate once one identifies the obscured theory that resolves the apparent contradiction. In his article "A Soldier and Afeard,"[2] Paul Cantor observes that for a "courageous man," Macbeth is unusually prone to moments of extreme fear (296), and he attributes this quality to the conflicting influences of paganism and Christianity. Macbeth is a pagan warrior tormented by a Christian conscience (294). In "Source and Motive in *Macbeth* and *Othello*,"[3] E. E. Stoll argues that Macbeth's character is intentionally "unpsychological." Shakespeare has created a contradictory character because he recognizes that dramatic tension is inherent in the narrative of a "good man doing the deed of horror" (320). E. K. Chambers asserts that a good man can be "completely overmastered by mysterious and inexplicable temptation"[4], and J.I.M. Stewart[5] contends that there are two irreconcilable Macbeths, one before the murder of Duncan, the other after. Macbeth commits the murder while still dazed from battle, entering the King's chamber in a blood-drenched delirium.

Marjorie Garber's explanation of the tragic hero's behavior most closely resembles that which I will offer here. Employing Freud's theory of the "uncanny," she describes Shakespeare's play as a "parade of forbidden images gazed on in peril".⁶ The uncanny is a "morbid anxiety," resulting when a repressed object or idea reemerges to trouble the conscious mind (87). In this case, the image of murder and particularly regicide arises to shake Macbeth's inner peace. Julia Kristeva's theory of abjection⁷ goes further in elucidating Macbeth's mercurial behavior. Like the uncanny, abjection attempts to explain the discomfort one experiences when confronted with the repressed. However, Kristeva embeds abjection within the process of identity formation. The abject is a requisite part of subjectivity, that which was appropriated in the binary construction of consciousness, that which defines the subject through opposition: "an Other who precedes and possesses me, and through such possession causes me to be" (10). For Kristeva, subjectivity is formed through a series expulsions, rejections of the "not self." Horror is experienced when the individual is confronted by the sudden manifestation of those qualities which were rejected in the formation of subjectivity: "the abject has only one quality of the object—that of being opposed to it" (1).

The theory of abjection as I will apply it to Shakespeare's *Macbeth* necessitates a medieval world view, an ideology that regards patriotism and allegiance as a sacred duty, the breach of which constitutes a transgression of boundaries that define the subjectivity of a subject or the conscience and consciousness of the King's vassal. Macbeth's self-image is constructed upon a medieval concept of loyalty to the monarch, the violation of which brings catastrophe to portions of the cosmos far removed from humanity: darkness to the surface of the earth, devastating winds, disruptions within the animal kingdom, etc.. Within such a context, Macbeth's psychic meltdown, before, during, and immediately after his "most sacrilegious murder" of the king, approaches the explicable. Macbeth is not a rebel and a regicide, but the scourge of rebels and regicides, so when he commits the single most meaningful [un]defining act for a patriot, he experiences a profound dissociative experience, an identity rupture manifest in hyperbolic speech, hallucinations, and hysteria. Felicity Rosslyn has defined this struggle as the effort "to keep out of consciousness the mixed nature of reality".⁸

The opening paradoxes of the witches prepare the audience for Macbeth's transformation. The assertion that "Fair is foul, and foul is fair" (I, i, 11) reveals the complicated relationship between the subject and the abject. Because selfhood is generated through opposition to the abject, the latter is vital to the former, marking off the boundaries where "meaning collapses" (Kristeva 2). Thus, the witches eulogize the passing of neatly defined borders within the play: women become men; nobles become kings; patriots become rebels; friends and kinsmen, enemies; guests, victims; children, combatants; princes, vagabonds; and the future, the present. Of course, the transformation that is of most interest to this discussion is Macbeth's own.

Beginning with the witches' observation that he will be king, Macbeth registers a horror which seems inappropriate to the auspicious pronouncement: A...why do you start and seem to fear/ Things that do sound so fair@ (I.iii.51-52). Macbeth's first soliloquy exposes not only shock and disbelief, but also a recognition of the moral ambiguity of his predicament and the necessity of realizing his good fortune through self-annihilating violence. The fulfillment of the first prophecy makes his heart pound and his hair stand on end, a reaction that reveals a combination of revulsion and fascination; he struggles against contrary emotions: "terror and excitement and dread and ambition" (Rosslyn 13). However, his present panic is insubstantial compared to the abject horror that accompanies the fantasy of murdering the king. Regicide is an act that he cannot countenance or even name:

My thought, whose murder yet is but fantastical,
Shakes so my single state of man that function
Is smothered in surmise, and nothing is
But what is not. (I.iii.139-142)

The medieval postulate that the human body is a microcosm of the world contains a subtle acknowledgment of the disruption that his ascent to power necessitates. The order of the state is established and maintained by the king who signifies rationality. Here Macbeth's imaginary disorder includes a collapse of rational government and the devolution of the state into its antithesis—chaos. However, the correspondent body is likewise convulsed. Macbeth inaugurates the beginning of his obsession with advancement, but appropriately, he cannot name that which he desires. He recognizes that his metamorphosis will require a revolution for the micro and macrocosms, a peripeteia and a translation of subject into abject: "...nothing is, but what is not."

Lady Macbeth experiences a similar aversion to that of her husband. She can name Glamis and Cawdor, but she will not name "king," referring to it awkwardly as "...What thou art promised" (I.v.17). She chastises the messenger who announces the king's imminent arrival: "Thou art mad to say it" (I.v.32). Her outburst reveals disbelief at her good fortune (Duncan will be under her power), but it also captures a moment of confusion in which she assumes the messenger has referred to Macbeth as "king." She is reticent to crown Macbeth with words; her ambition lies beyond naming.

As Macbeth considers the consequences of his treasonous actions, he collides once again with the abject. He associates the potential murder of the King with a revolutionary restructuring of his character. His ambition necessitates that he "o'erleap" himself, becoming that which he is not, that which he cannot name or countenance. His crime violates his obligation to medieval order and degree, to civilization. He must violate the obligatory social contracts dictating passive obedience to kings, kindness to kinsmen, and protection to guests. The transgression of social obligation necessitates that he redefine himself as a traitor and a villain outside of culture, a self that is radically excluded from nature, court, and good will. He assumes that his deed will instigate apocalyptic catastrophe, blowing "the horrid deed in every eye" (I.vii.24), an allusion to the universality of tragic repercussions as well as the inevitability of discovery and universal scorn.

Kristeva recognizes that the formation of subjectivity is ongoing. Expulsion is not final; the abject "does not stop separating" (8). It returns periodically manifesting itself as revulsion and loathing (10). The structure of the Kristeva theory, of course, resembles the psychomachia of the medieval morality structure, a clash of polarities, one compliance and one revolution. The recognition of Macbeth's inner struggle is not a unique insight, but the extent to which it determines subjectivity may be. His reticence reveals a self-designing impulse. He fears exposure not because he dreads punishment, but because he wishes to evade odium and humiliation. He wishes to wear "golden opinions" bought "from all sorts of people" (I.vii.33). The goodwill of others is a portion of his patriotic self-image, and his spurning of good opinion haunts him because he was obliged to sacrifice the "troops of friends" who attend old age. Even after he has committed regicide, he is still concerned about his public image. He explains to the murderers of Banquo that he must conceal his involvement because he does not wish to lose the friends that he and the victim share. The odium of others is not all the punishment that he must endure. The loathing becomes internalized; for a time he suffers pangs of conscience, obviating the continued rupture of the subject and abject binary. Macbeth admits that he has 'defiled' his mind, and "Put rancors in the vessel of ...[his] peace" (III.i.65 and 67), and only after he has become hardened through reiterated crimes and auspicious prophecies does he escapes conscience.

The desperate need for concealment constitutes a motif within the drama. Macbeth and his wife repeatedly invoke darkness to hide their crimes from human and heavenly justice, but their parallel concern is the clarity of their own consciences. The eye must "wink at the hand," not to acknowledge a silent complicity, but to hide the transgression from its perpetrator. Macbeth first summons darkness following the pronouncement of Malcolm's succession to the throne. Furious that he was not named and recognizing that he is still further from the "golden round," he commands the stars to hide their fires, thus concealing his "black and deep desires." Only Macbeth could be privy to his "deep desires" unless he decides to share them. He admits that he fears to see that which the hand will perpetrate, yet he yearns for the glorious outcome.

In his second effort to muster darkness, he achieves a greater distance from his crime. Night itself will crush Banquo and depart, leaving Macbeth a clear conscience. Lady Macbeth also commands the night:

> Come, thick night,
> And pall thee in the dunnest smoke of Hell,
> That my keen knife see not the wound it makes,
> Nor Heaven peep through the blanket of the dark...
> (I.v.51-4)

Despite the murderous resolution that she later demonstrates, Lady Macbeth, like her husband, prefers to wink at her own crimes. She understands the necessity of overcoming her own nature in order to transact her "bloody business." She must undergo a translation into her antithesis, adopting masculine traits and stopping the "access and passage to remorse" (I.v.45).

Macbeth's behavior during and after the murder of Duncan reveals the horror of abjection. The troubling prospect of murdering the King momentarily motivates Macbeth to abandon his plans, a decision which provokes recriminations from his wife. The ensuing debate over the composition of manhood confuses the binary structure of subject and abject. Macbeth asserts that he "dare[s] do all that would become a man./Who dares do more is none" (I.vii.46-7), thus defining manhood as honor and virtue, as remaining within the scope of the socially determined propriety. Those who break the social contract that dictates civility are monsters or beasts, not men.[9] The monstrous transcends the villainy, provoking horror and necessitating an appropriation of that which is inimical to the subject. The seduction by his wife relates to his personal identity, how he will understand himself if he becomes a regicide. Lady Macbeth disagrees with her husband's characterization of manhood, maintaining that it is resolution and daring, not obedience and compunction. He will become a greater man (literally and figuratively) should he follow through with his murderous action. Her theory of the subject commandeers the abject offering it as an alternative for consumption, an idea that adds new meaning to Macbeth's assertion that he has "supp'd full with horror" (V.vi.13). It seems, however, that Lady Macbeth's plot convinces more than her argument.

Macbeth is appalled during and after his violent episodes. He requires supernatural prompting in order to initiate the murder of Duncan. Both the air-drawn dagger and the image of Traquin's ravishing strides suggest a dissociative experience in which Macbeth is outside himself watching as he commits an irrational and unacceptable act. Roman Polanski's filmic production of the scene[10] enhances the madness of the moment by adopting the perspective of the killer, blurring the image and speeding up the camera. The effect replicates delirium and dissociation. Of course, madness does not allow Macbeth to escape the horror of the moment, and the fallout of his crime is immediate as he takes stock of the multiple covenants that he has profaned. He is now a masterless man without guidance of conscience or reason.[11] He has separated himself from God and cannot expect blessing: "amen stuck in my throat" (II.ii.32). He has violated the natural order, and even Neptune's ocean is complicit in his condemnation. Most importantly he has ruptured his own inner peace with "most admired disorder." His revulsion is abjection; he cannot assimilate his act into his self-image: "I am afraid to think what I have done,/Look on it again I dare not" (II.ii.51-2). At the conclusion of the murder scene, he reveals the extent to which he is unable to assimilate his actions into his self-image: "To know my deed, 't'were best not know myself" (II.ii.73). Macbeth equivocates when responding to the discovery of Duncan's body. He appears to eulogize the King, acknowledging the wickedness of the age and the disruption of the social and natural orders; however, the occulted subject of his diatribe is self-laceration:

> Had I but died an hour before the chance,
> I had lived a blessed time, for from this instant
> There's nothing serious in mortality.
> All is but toys. Renown and grace is dead....
> (II.iii.96-99)

Macbeth laments the passing of his reputation and his honor, and it is indeed true that if he had died before Duncan's murder, he would have "lived a blessed time."

In the murder of Banquo and the slaughter of Macduff's family, Macbeth tries to distance himself physically and morally from the crimes, revealing a continued effort to hide his transgressions from himself (Cantor 305). He suborns murderers in both cases. However, the effort to detach himself from the crime is ineffective. The appearance of Banquo's ghost initiates the most dramatic manifestation of Macbeth's bad conscience. In his article "A Soldier and Afeard," Paul Cantor argues that Macbeth's histrionics result from his fear of the supernatural not from any earthly powers (295). This position does not seem consistent with other events within the drama, particularly Macbeth's visit to the witches. When given a chance to hear the supernatural predictions either from the witches or from their demonic master Hecate, Macbeth chooses the latter. It is equally improbable that he responds entirely to the ghost's "gory locks," since he has a reputation for his bloodthirsty performances on the battlefield. Instead, he reacts to the accusation of murder embodied in the ghost, denying involvement: "Thou canst not say I did it" (III.iv.50). The ghost's two visitations within the scene punctuate Macbeth's effort to characterize himself as a thoughtful, well-meaning king and kinsman. Each entrance follows

Macbeth's hypocritical efforts to feign disappointment at Banquo's absence. Kristeva associates the horror of death and the dead with abjection (3), and for Macbeth, the ghost also fractures the self-perceived unity of his character, mocking the self that he performs for himself and the world. Once his guests have departed, he voices his concern with the discovery of his crimes and rationalizes his self-destructive fears: "My strange and self-abuse/Is the initiate fear that wants hard use./We are but young in deed" (III.iv.142-44). The prediction that he will acclimate himself to murder turns out to be truer that he might have intended.

Of course the ultimate act of self-overcoming for Macbeth is the murder of Macduff's family. While initially he tries to detach himself from the action and the subsequent compunction, a sign that he is still concerned with his self-image and the approval of others, he, nevertheless, concludes by abandoning all pretense of virtue and wallowing in villainy. He is translated into the abject, reconciling his infamy with his martial valor. Like the rebel Cawdor, he "labored in his country's wreck." When he proudly puts on his armor before the final battle with Malcolm and Macduff, Macbeth is symbolically shielding himself from the remorse that tormented him when he still harbored an idealistic self-image. The armor symbolically guards him from the news of his wife's death which does not appear to shake him inordinately. Having sustained himself with horrors for a prolonged period and having confronted and assimilated the specter of his "slaughterous thoughts," he has no expectation of honor or heaven, so "night shrieks" no longer "start" him, as he has little to fear that he has not already confronted. Lady Macbeth's death does little more than inspire ruminations into the absurdity of life. The resulting soliloquy appropriately acknowledges the futility of human aspirations and the constructedness of subjectivity. As "poor players," humanity has no unified identity but only a series of meaningless roles that express us to the world. Macbeth's assertion that life is "a tale/ Told by an idiot, full of sound and fury,/Signifying nothing" (V.v.26-8) reveals the collapse of binary structures that generate subjectivity and meaning. Macbeth recognizes that horrors always were a part of him, that the not self is as central to subjectivity as the self.

Macbeth is the true heart of darkness; he has kicked himself loose of the earth and can be appealed to in the name of nothing either high or low. The medieval social and moral structure that appropriates horror and revulsion as a deterrents to ambition and regicide is a construct, requiring the constant repudiation of the "not self." Within the medieval cosmology, treason is the ultimate collapse of the negotiation between self and other, between patriotism and regicide, between champion and villain. While the abject must be internalized, it must also be governed. Macbeth's seeming disunity dramatizes the contest between the good and the bad conscience, a struggle familiar to the medieval world.

*MISSISSIPPI UNIVERSITY FOR WOMEN*

NOTES

[1] All quotations from the play are from William Shakespeare, *Macbeth*, in *Shakespeare: The Complete Works*, ed. G.B. Harrison (New York: Harcourt Brace, 1952): 1184-1218.
[2] Paul Cantor, "A Soldier and Afeard: Macbeth and the Gospelling of Scotland," in *Interpretation* 14 (1997): 287-318.
[3] E.E. Stoll, "Source and Motive in *Macbeth* and *Othello*," in *Shakespeare: Modern Essays in Criticism*, ed. Leonard Dean (London: Oxford UP, 1957): 317-328.
[4] Quoted in J.I.M. Stewart, "Steep Tragic Contrast: *Macbeth*," in *Shakespeare: The Late Tragedies*, ed. Clifford Leech (Chicago: U of Chicago P, 1965), 102-120, (112).
[5] Ibid., 113.
[6] Marjorie Garber, "*Macbeth*: The Male Medusa," in *Shakespeare's Late Tragedies: A Collection of Critical Essays*, ed. Susanne L. Wofford (Upper Saddle River, NJ: Prentice Hall, 1996): 74-103, (80).
[7] Julia Kristeva, *The Powers of Horror: An Essay on Abjection*, trans. Leon S. Roudiez (New York: Columbia UP, 1982).
[8] Felicity Rosslyn, "Villainy, Virtue, and Projection," in *The Cambridge Quarterly* 30 (2001): 2-17 (15).
[9] Eugene Waith, "Manhood and Valor in Two Shakespearean Tragedies," in *English Literary History* 30 (1950): 265-68 (264), 3.
[10] *Macbeth*, director Roman Polanski, (Columbia Pictures, 1971).
[11] Steven Mullaney, "Lying Like Truth: Riddle, Representation, and Treason in Renaissance England," in *English Literary History* 47 (1980): 32-47 (34).

Searching for God and Arthur:
Jim Hunter's
*Percival and the Presence of God*

Peter G. Christensen

Jim Hunter's novel *Percival and the Presence of God* (1978)[1] is significant as one of the very few English-language treatments of the Percival story in the last thirty years which can compete in artistic quality with works in German and French from the same period, such as the films of Eric Rohmer and Hans-Jürgen Syberberg. It has been interpreted as a "Christian existentialist novel" by Raymond H. Thompson, who interviewed Hunter at his home in England in 1989. Thompson wrote the Introduction for the reprint edition in 1997 and discussed the novel in his survey article "The Grail in Modern Fiction" in *The Grail: A Casebook* (2000).[2] Hunter, in his interview with Thompson, encouraged this categorization as a "Christian existentialist novel,"[3] but the term seems at odds with the novel's epigraph by Iris Murdoch, who is commenting on Dietrich Bonhoeffer, a Christian, in order to disagree with him. After a review of criticism of the novel and a brief plot summary, I will go on to argue that *Percival and the Presence of God* is indeed a "Christian existentialist novel," not through its open connections with Murdoch and Bonhoeffer, but through its affinities to Kierkegaard, its inscription in a tradition of British poetry stretching back to *Sir Gawain and the Green Knight*, and its departures from the works of Chrétien de Troyes and Wolfram von Eschenbach.

The setting of *Percival and the Presence of God* lends itself to symbolic readings. Norris J. Lacy and Geoffrey Ashe place the novel among "novels set in the Middle Ages along with those by Vera Chapman…Richard Monaco, Phyllis Ann Karr, and T. H. White,"[4] but, as Thompson points out,[5] Hunter's is really very different from theirs, as its setting is actually very vague. Beverly Taylor and Elisabeth Brewer[6] in their brief discussion of the novel in *The Return of King Arthur* imply that the novel's meaning is connected to the scene in the Grail castle: "Not even to question why suffering is experienced is in a sense to condone it. Such acceptance allows the pain to be perpetuated, to be endlessly repeated, and perhaps we are meant to see an allusion to modern indifference here." Taylor and Brewer do not appear to consider Hunter's novel "existentialist," and so perhaps "existentialist" may be a confusing label for it. The question of the existential content of the novel is connected to the individual reader's interpretation of the meaning of what Hunter refers to as the "code." Alan Lupack[7] sees the code as directing Percival to pursue the Fisher Lord, but I see his quest to be in opposition to the code and thus more existential and antinomian.

As there are varieties of Christian existentialism, the term "Christian existentialist novel" may suggest a work influenced by various religious figures: Kierkegaard, Dostoevsky, or Berdayev, for instance. For Thompson, categorization of the novel is connected to the most striking sentence in the novel, spoken by the first-person protagonist Percival near the end of his adventures: "I no longer believe in Arthur, it being all I can manage to believe in God."[8]

To make the Grail story more contemporary to twentieth-century religious concerns, Hunter offers an enormously stripped-down version of Chrétien's and Wolfram's poems—the type of change that can make a fable from a complicated allegory. In this bare-bones version of the story, the plot is easy to follow. The novel's twelve chapters easily fall into three sets of four chapters. The first three chapters cover only a single day in which Percival, with local help, defeats a dozen brigands who have attacked the castle of Whiteflower while her husband is away. He becomes her lover, and he has the dead men burned rather than left to be eaten by wolves, an action according to the Arthurian code of behavior that reflects respect for human life.

At the beginning of the third chapter, we are given indications that Percival has been out in the world for two years telling his story. He rapidly summarizes of the events up to the end of Chapter 9, when he leaves the Grail Castle. Chapters 4-6 reveal the events of the winter that Percival spends with Whiteflower as her lover while her husband is away, presumably dead. The next three chapters treat the adventures at the Grail Castle of Henged, the wounded Fisher King, and Percival's discovery that everyone has disappeared when he awakens from troubled dreams the day after the ritual. The last three chapters show Percival on his confused journey to find Arthur. He narrowly avoids freezing to death in a ruined Chapel Perilous, and he is rescued.

Whereas it is usually harder for a person to believe in the existence of God rather than a certain human being, here Percival finds it harder to confirm or refute the existence of a man Arthur, who is supposed to live fairly close by. In this novel, Arthur may not exist, and his adventures in the minds of the people seem to blend with those of other legendary and/or possibly real men. The novel's conclusion shows Percival resuming the quest for the Fisher King rather than for Arthur, whom he had originally sought. Hunter, by the end of the novel, places the existence of King Arthur in the category of hearsay, whereas the existence of God is based on his evaluation of his own personal feelings. For Percival, it makes more sense to believe an inner feeling about God than a general report about the reality of Arthur.

Although I do think, like Thompson, that *Percival and the Presence of God* is a Christian existentialist novel, I will try to show that it is so in a different sense—through its relationship to Kierkegaard rather than Bonhoeffer. In his interview, Hunter never seems to realize that his Percival is a version of the knight of faith in Kierkegaard's *Fear and Trembling* rather than a literary descendant of Beckett and Camus as he claims (8). Unlike Chrétien's and Wolfram's Percivals, Hunter's hero neither arrives at Arthur's court nor returns to the Grail Castle, which he visited once. He abandons the search for Arthur and his court of secular noble virtue, and insists on trying to find the Grail Castle again to attempt to heal Henged (the Fisher King), even though he can barely believe that God exists.

The epigraph, taken from the writings of Iris Murdoch, suggests that we should live as if God does not exist. This idea of what we might call 'bracketing out God' and going on with daily life hardly seems to be the same thing as Hunter advocates. Hunter's Percival goes on a strange, antisocial quest where he can perform a single great act of compassion if and only if the journey is finally completed. Hunter quotes Murdoch as follows:

> When Bonhoeffer says that God wants us to live as if there were no God I suspect he is misusing words....We are simply here. And if there is any kind of sense or unity in human life, and the dream of this does not cease to haunt us, it is of some other kind and must be sought within a human experience which has nothing outside it. (xv)

It is easy enough to trace this quotation to "The Sovereignty of Good over Other Concepts,"[9] the 1967 Leslie Stephen Lecture. In the context of the entire lecture, we find that Murdoch is critical of existentialism, including Christian existentialism, and that she is not rephrasing Bonhoeffer in order to agree with him but rather to clarify his thought for her audience so as to disagree with him. Murdoch had criticized existentialism in many essays since 1950, and in the late 1960s she began to develop her own ethical system strongly indebted to Plato's ideas on the Good and the Beautiful.

Perhaps Hunter had been attracted to the quotation because of the sentence before it, where Murdoch claims that "human life has no external point or _____." (365). This belief does give her something in common with existentialist thinkers, but it does not make her an existentialist. As Peter Conardi points out in the Preface to Murdoch's philosophical essays, collected in 1997, despite her appreciation for Kierkegaard's large role in the development of modern religious psychology, "she cannot but think him 'tiresome' and 'queer'" (xiv). She finds in existentialism a version of Romanticism that overstresses the will, and she does not feel that it is individual choice which creates value, even when we have moments when we feel we are radically alienated. In this existential world that Murdoch wishes to avoid:

> Values which were previously in some sense inscribed in the heavens and guaranteed by God collapse into the human will. There is no

transcendent reality. The idea of the good remains indefinable and empty so that human choice may fill it. The sovereign moral concept is freedom, or possibly courage in a sense which identifies it with freedom, will, power. (366)

Murdoch is suspicious of alienated loners and has considered and rejected the view that existentialism is a self-serving rejection of Marxism, which generalizes the bourgeois sense of alienation into a general human condition. In any case, a return to the Platonic notion of the Good is for her a better approach than Marxism to post-Kantian romantic philosophy.

The religious work lurking in the background of Hunter's novel is Kierkegaard's *Fear and Trembling*,[10] a book which would constitute for Murdoch a high point of egotistical Romanticism in philosophy. As Brita K. Stendahl[11] says of Kierkegaard's highest state, the religious:

By doing our duty, we fulfill the requirements of state, church, and family. We pay our taxes, obey the laws, honor our family tradition, and keep the commandments. But in doing our duty, we do not get into a relationship with God. In faith, however, there exists a relationship between an individual and God that stretches beyond normal duties. In such a relationship, the individual is absolutely on his own—not the norm, but the exception. (120-21)

Kierkegaard answers in the affirmative to the question, "Is there an absolute Duty to God?" [Gives der en absolute Plig: mod Gud?"][12], and he posits the teleological suspension of the ethical in one's absolute duty to God.

At the very beginning of Problemata I in *Fear and Trembling*, Kierkegaard made this point about the teleological suspension of the ethical:

The ethical as such is the universal, and as the universal it applies to everyone, which from another angle means that it applies at all times. It rests immanent in itself, has nothing outside itself that is its $f≠^aø¬$ [end, purpose] but is itself the $f≠^aø¬$ for everything outside itself, and when the ethical has absorbed this into itself, it goes not further. (54)

Hunter's Percival ultimately replaces an externalized socially approved quest (desire to find Arthur at his court) for an individualized interior summons to do a deed which has no claim on others (return to Henged). It is a version of the absolute duty to God. By throwing out almost all of the concrete Arthurian settings and familial relations presented by Chrétien and Wolfram, Hunter creates an almost timeless world in which interiorized goals are valorized, given that the loss of transcendental meaning (absence of God) is always a possibility. Percival's knight of faith may be unhorsed the next time disaster strikes.

At the end of the novel, when fearing that no rescue is in sight, Percival thinks:

God wasn't with me. As the pain beat out of the darkness again to overwhelm any other impression, I couldn't feel sure that God had ever been with me—not even a malicious God. Nothing as intimate and human as malice seemed carried on the largeness of the night or the insistence of that pain. They spoke either of an immense and grand cruelty, or of a vast indifference. Percival was simply not of interest to God. (148)

This Percival is not connected to the Grail community by either family ties with the Fisher King or participation in a community like the Knights Templar. He is on his own.

As Hunter's Percival does not have Wolfram's hero's sins on his conscience, so we as readers can be sympathetic to what his inner voice tells him to do. Wolfram's Parzival had killed a relative and robbed the latter's armor. Furthermore, he has neglected his mother, who comes to die of a broken heart.[13] By reducing greatly Percival's sins, Hunter makes it easier for us to accept the complete separation of the Arthurian world and the spiritual world. As Hunter himself points out in the interview, the novel's setting is nebulous in time and place, and it cannot really be a part of the High Middle Age. Noticeably absent is what Will Hasty finds to be Wolfram's "concern with morality in chivalry."[14] There is no chivalry in the most widely accepted sense even visible—just a code of conduct and glimmerings of a feudal world. The code has a long history. Geoffrey of Monmouth says that Arthur "established such a code of courtliness in his household that he inspired peoples living far away to imitate him".[15]

Percival puts aside his desire to get to join Arthur's service and his hope to find again either his mother or his mistress Whiteflower. These goals are replaced by a personal conviction that he can help heal Henged by speaking up, a view for which absolutely no one can offer him confirmation.[16] His inability to believe in Arthur when he has all he can do to believe in God is a memorable statement, but it requires him to assume that everyone around him has been either deluded or lying about Arthur's existence. To reject Arthur for Henged is an intensely personal intuitive choice, since God is never directly connected to the ritual at the Grail Castle by anyone at the Castle and since, previously, his strongest sense of God came from sexual intercourse with Whiteflower.

Hunter's Percival is a knight of faith who has made the teleological suspension of the ethical. After he leaves the mysteriously vacated Grail castle, he looks to God for a higher justification than the ethical code provides. He may seem mad to those who come in contact with him, but he is the determiner of his own values. His goal seems absurd to others. Hunter brings in the word "absurd" and its derivatives several times at the end of the novel (149, 151,

156, 157), as well as "nothing" (148), and "God's indifference" (151). His feelings that everything may be absurd are temporarily pushed aside when he hopes to be rescued in the nick of time from freezing to death in what may be the ruins of Arthur's chapel, a ruin where a falling beam has immobilized him by breaking his leg (151). Since the girl who finds him appears to be incapable of comprehension, he falls into the "absurd" again when she goes away. Fortunately, she does eventually bring help. In the end, although Percival sees himself as an example of self-sacrifice on behalf of the Fisher King (164) and as a person who will teach Arthur's code to boys, it may just be wishful thinking (194-65).

Confronted by the alternatives of an arbitrary world and the "haphazardness of God," his choice of God's haphazardness indicates that God is no longer at the heart of what Murdoch would call the Good. Percival has retreated into a world of romantic privacy that can be self-serving. Percival replaces the code, representative of normal social ethics of a high moral standard, with the internal goal indicated by the cup and sword at the castle of Henged the Fisher King, two objects that appear symbolically Christian.

In Hunter's novel, following the advice of a friendly abbot, who counseled him to listen, receive, and observe (115), Percival had kept silent, watching the miracle of the blood pulsing out of the spear point into the cup (118-19). Since the novel does not explain the origins of the Grail or what it signifies, the reader feels that Percival's decision to remain silent during the miracle is just as reasonable as his interruption of the ritual to ask a question or say something. Only through his own increasing religious revelation does he feel that he did the wrong thing. No character tells him so, nor is his silence caused by any previous misdeed. No one prompts him to conclude, as he does, that the abbot's advice was "wrong" (168). In Hunter's world, however, it is "wrong," not because it is unethical but because it has no relevance to the internalized voice of the divine.[17]

The Kierkegaardian element in *Percival and the Presence of God* is not mentioned in the information that Hunter provided to Raymond Thompson in their interview conducted on May 20, 1989 at Wickhambreux, Kent. However, I do not feel that it makes this connection any less crucial. In the interview, Hunter indicates that he is not an expert on Arthurian materials. Nor is he a medievalist or anthropologist. His research into the Holy Grail for his novel was relatively limited, although he did read Chrétien de Troyes and at least part of *Parzival* by Wolfram von Eschenbach.

Hunter says in the interview that he chose Percival rather than Galahad as his hero because of his Quaker and pacifist upbringing, and his concern with compassion. When Hunter says that Percival is "trapped by his destiny" (7), I cannot agree, since only the legend and nothing in the novel itself points to Percival as someone "chosen" to relieve the suffering of the Fisher King. If Hunter means that his hero is trapped in the destiny that he has inherited from Chrétien and Wolfram, this is a different sense of destiny altogether.

On the subject of Christianity in the novel, Hunter told Thompson, "For me and a number of readers, the book deals with the relationship with Christianity, and Christians tend to find the book particularly moving" (8). The reader is challenged to ask if God is present (8). Hunter compares his novel to the "works, of, say, Camus or Beckett, or someone like that, written in a Christian context" (8). However, I believe that Camus or Beckett 'in a Christian context' would not seem much like Camus or Beckett. Hunter avoids stating whether he has Christian faith or not, and he does not make any claim to be promoting Christianity in the novel.

Hunter in the interview names several famous works of literature from which he has borrowed elements in his novel. However, we should not conclude that, because we can find similarities in the tone of these works, they carry the same message. Among the specific references are Coleridge's "The Rime of the Ancient Mariner," T. S. Eliot's *The Waste Land* and "The Journey of the Magi," Robert Browning's "Childe Roland to the Dark Tower Came," as well as the Pearl-Poet's *Sir Gawain and the Green Knight*.

Looking more closely at these figures, we see that Hunter's Percival has a compulsion to tell his tale like the Ancient Mariner or to reflect on it like Eliot's Magus, and like the Magus, Childe Roland, and the Green Knight, he passes through Waste Lands. Coleridge writes, near the end of the poem and after the Mariner's horrible voyage is over, that he must find release by telling his tale:

> Since then, at an uncertain hour,
> That agony returns;
> And till my ghastly tale is told,
> This hour within me burns.[18] (581-85)

Similarly, Percival interrupts the description of his taking Whiteflower as his mistress to tell of his compulsion to narrate his tale. In a crucial passage which appears after Percival has sex with Whiteflower, he states, "For nearly two years I have been telling the same story: the true story. More briefly than here, for now I'm telling it to myself as well as to you in a hope of understanding" (30). Percival's double audience of self and other is very reminiscent of the Mariner's.

The Magus in Eliot's "Journey of the Magi" has committed no misdeed, but he has about him the same feelings of confusion as Percival and the Mariner:

> But there was no information, and so we continued
> And arrived at evening, not a moment too soon

Finding the places; it was (you may say) satisfactory.[19](29-31)

Although Hunter's Percival travels alone, in his journey Hunter picks up Eliot's use of the word "satisfactory":

> There were nine hours of daylight, in which to travel. That first day proved more or less satisfactory: I wasn't cold, in the grey drizzle, as long as I kept moving, and in spite of my impatience I kept my horse to a steady pace, at which he can continue all day. Wet pastures of early winter, bushes and trees almost bare, brown bran-mash of leaves and mud beside the track. To my right, the grey shadows of the land moving up into low cloud, with no sign of the ridge-tops. (135)

Even the rhythm of the words here seems deliberately Eliotic. Percival, like the Magi "no longer at ease," as Eliot says, cannot go back to his previous life. Like the Magi who have a hint of Christ's sufferings, Percival's knowledge of Henged's sufferings initiates his changed worldview. This Percival may also be considered "throbbing between two lives," like Tiresias in Eliot's *The Waste Land*[20] (218).

Eliot's Waste Land motif is also visible in Browning's 1855 "Childe Roland to the Dark Tower Came"[21] as in Stanza XXVI:

> Now blotches rankling, coloured gay and grim,
>    Now patches where some leanness of the soil's
>    Broke into moss or substances like boils;
> Then came some palsied oak, a cleft in him
>    Like a distorted mouth that splits its rim
>    Gaping at death, and dies while it recoils. (150-56)

As a teacher of English literature at prep schools for many years, Hunter is well aware of the tradition into which he has tapped for his heroes traveling through a hostile, barren land.

Hunter sends Percival thorough snowy landscapes, and here he may have been reminded specifically of thee opening of the Fourth Fitt of *Sir Gawain and the Green Knight*[22]

> Now neghez the New Yere, and nyght passez,
> The day dryvez to the derk, as Dryghtyn biddez;
> Bot wylde wederez of the worlde wakned theroute,
> Clowdes kesten kenly the colde to the erthe,
> Wyth nyghe innoghe of the northe the naked to tene.
> The snawe snitered ful smart, that snayped the wylde;
> The werbelande wynde wapped fro the hyghe,
> And drof uche dale ful of dryftes ful grete. (4. 1998-2005)

The ending of *Sir Gawain and the Green Knight* offers more resolution than does Hunter's novel. The quest is completed and Gawain returns to Arthur's court. Hunter's Percival neither starts from nor returns to Arthur's court. The girdle indicates Gawain's reintegration into society, but Hunter's hero wants no such reintegration.

Hunter's Christian existentialist interpretation of the Grail procession is consolidated by the reworking of the motif of the Bleeding Cup and Lance, so suggestive of the Crucifixion although it is not specifically mentioned. His description of the Grail is not copied from either of the two classic accounts. For example, Chrétien writes (in Nigel Bryant's translation[23]):

> While they were talking of one thing and another, a boy came from a chamber clutching a white lance by the middle of the shaft, and passed between the fire and the two who were sitting on the bed. Everyone in the hall saw the white lance with its white head; and a drop of blood issued from the tip of the lance's head, and right down to the boy's hand this red drop ran. The lord's guest gazed at this marvel that had appeared there that night, but restrained himself from asking how it came to be, because he remembered the advice of the nobleman who had made him a knight, who had taught and instructed him to beware of talking too much; he feared it would be considered base of him if he asked, so he did not. (35)

In Chrétien's account, as compared to Hunter's, there is less a connection between the lance ("une blanche lance" line 58, p.156)[24] and the cup and the Grail. In fact, Chrétien does not directly connect the Bleeding Lance and the Grail, and Chrétien's Grail is not like Hunter's cup, since Chrétien's Grail appears as a somewhat ordinary serving dish for a rich man.

Hunter's description is even less close to Wolfram's parallel scene, in which a page brings in a sword which the lord awards to Parzival, telling him (in A. T. Hatto's translation), "Whenever you put it to the test in battle it will stand you in good stead".[25] Wolfram immediately laments Parzival's silence:

> Alas that he asked no Question then! Even now I am cast down on his account! For when he was given the sword it was to prompt him to ask a Question! I mourn too for his gentle host, who is dogged by misfortune from on high of which he could be rid by a Question. (127)

Hunter's Parzifal is more emotionally involved in the scene, since he notes that Henged's "eyes were half-open now, again looking into the hall." He uses empathy and thinks that within Henged's "head was silence, pain-gripped, a soundless state" (115). Our modern hero is given no sword whose hilt was like a ruby (sÓn gehilze was ein rubÓn, stanza 239, 21). There is no visible sense of his election. It is more internalized and private than in Wolfram's poem.

As Justin E. Griffin points out in *The Holy Grail*,[26] "All the Grail hero must do to achieve the Grail is to ask the question and inquire about the mysterious relic. Therefore, all who undertake the task of understanding the Grail immediately find what they are seeking." Hunter's Percival is not concerned with what the Grail actually is, in the sense of whether it is a cup that received Christ's blood or the cup from the Last Supper. He does not wonder about it, although the bleeding lance that drips into the cup probably suggests that it is a cup that received Christ's blood. For Percival, eliminating Henged's suffering is what counts, not understanding the nature of the Grail or its mystery *per se* (163). The blending of sex and Christianity is greater in Hunter's novel than in the medieval romancers, since the Bleeding Lance and Cup signify intercourse and crucifixion at the same time, and they torment Percival when they are blended in his nightmares. Thus, the nightmare after the Grail ritual becomes a sexual nightmare.

How different Hunter's treatment of the nightmare is from Wolfram's, for example, is apparent when we look at the restless sleep of Wolfram's hero the night after the ritual.

> Parzival's dream was quilted through and through at the seam with sword-blows and beyond it with many fine lance-thrusts: for in his sleep he suffered no little distress from charges delivered at full gallop. Waking, he would have suffered death thirty times over rather than this, so ill did my lord Disquiet pay him. (130)

In Hunter's novel, where Percival has several disturbing dreams, it is not clear whether after he retires for the night he has sex with a girl in the Grail ceremony or whether he only fantasizes it. Her appearance is described as a temptation that reminds the reader of his sexual awakening with Whiteflower. During that troubled night at Henged's castle, Percival says, "even as I tried to pray, to shut my mind, my hands were hurrying, lifting the coverings to bring her in beside me, stroking and parting her legs. Then the night took her from me" (121).

This passage in *Percival and the Presence of God* is meant to remind us that Percival clearly felt the presence of God when he first met Whiteflower, whom he has since abandoned. Although Hunter admits that he got the name of Whiteflower from the episode featuring Blanchefleur in Chrétien's *Le Roman de Perceval ou le Conte du Graal*, he takes his own initiative to turn her into the hero's lover. Chrétien's hero remains chaste when Blanchefleur comes to his bed, but Hunter's hero enjoys a graphically described scene of intercourse with Whiteflower. Chrétien writes, "And he kissed her and held her fast in his arms, and drew her gently and softly under the coverlet. She let him kiss her, and I don't think it displeased her" (Chrétien 1990: 101, 103). Here Perceval is a chaste knight indeed, even though "Et celle suefre qu'il la beise, / Ne ne cuit pas qu'il li enuit" (1982: 23, lines 2042-2043). In contrast, Percival says of Whiteflower, "My lady lifted my hands away from her breasts, placed them herself back at my sides; and brought her own hands, softly, to my penis" (25). When he has intercourse with her, Percival states, "For a time I resisted the physical symbolism of the spiritual mystery, and was partly alarmed to have it on my tongue" (27). As he kisses her during intercourse, he thinks of the "wafer upon the tongue, at the First Communion" (927). In the end, even Whiteflower, who meant so much to him, is renounced as a goal, perhaps forgotten.

In 1978, when Percival pursued his interiorized goal, the heyday of existentialism was long gone, and, among the avant-garde, scorned as ridiculously humanistic and self-centered. The complete absence of political considerations, guaranteed by the vague landscape of the story, in Hunter's novel only makes its existentialism stand out more clearly. In contrast, at this time the continental European Parcivals never quested far away from the political arena.

As Ulrich Müller[27] points out, since 1978 (the year of Hunter's novel), Parcival has become visible in Europe in film and theatre through Rohmer's *Perceval le Gallois* (1979), Syberberg's *Parsifal* (1982), the *Graal/The,tre* of Jacques Roubaud/Florence Delay (1977-1981), Richard Blank's tv-play *Parzival*, Tankred Dorst and Ursula Ehler's play *Merlin* with its sequels *Der Wilde, Der nackte Mann* and *Parzival: Ein Szenarium*, Robert Wilson's *Parzival: Auf der anderen Seite des Sees* (Hamburg, 1987), Christoph Hein's *Die Ritter der Tafelrunde*, George Gruntz's *The Holy Grail of Joy and Jazz,* and Peter Handke's *Das Spiel vom Fragen oder Die Reise zum sonoren Land*. However, Müller lists only one important recent German novel about the hero: Adolf Muschg's *Der rote Ritter: Eine Geschichte von Parziv,l* (1993). He finds less important Michel Moorcock's *The War Hound and the World's Pain* (1981), Peter Vansittart's *Parzifal* (1990) and the tetralogy by Richard Monaco (1977-1985).

It may be that the fall of Communism and the end of hopes for democracy emerging from Communist parties has made the Perceval-Grail motif more relevant to central and eastern Europe than to the United States and the United Kingdom. American smug, self-congratulatory politics have nothing in common with the regrets of disillusioned Marxists. Hunter's novel of Percival is completely apolitical, and again we are reminded of Murdoch's positioning existentialism and Marxism in opposition to each other. Only time will tell if Hunter's novel will be followed by more existential angst in the wake of capitalist expansion, or whether the Anglo-American Grail Castle will come to have political resonances like its continental counterpart.

*CARDINAL STRITCH UNIVERSITY*

NOTES

[1] Jim Hunter, *Percival and the Presence of God,* (London: Faber and Faber, 1978). Reprinted with an introduction by Raymond F. Thompson (Oakland: Green Knight, 1997). All quotations are from this edition.

[2] Raymond H. Thompson, "The Grail in Modern Fiction: Sacred Symbol in a Secular Age," in *The Grail: A* Casebook, ed. Dhira B. Mahoney, (New York: Garland, 2000), 545-60. When the Pendragon Series of Arthurian Reprints was begun in 1997, Thompson, general editor of the series, chose Hunter's *Percival and the Presence of God* to initiate it. Published by Faber in 1978, and reviewed favorably by *The Daily Telegraph, New Statesman, The Guardian,* and the *Times Literary Supplement, Percival and the Presence of God* had since been little noted and little distributed in the U. S. Some of the neglect may stem from the fact that Hunter, who has anthologized modern poetry and fiction and written a study of Tom Stoppard's plays, has not made any other contributions to Arthurian fiction. Indeed, *Percival and the Presence of God* seems to be the last novel he has published. In 1978, Hunter, born 24 June 1939, was already the author of seven volumes of fiction (all but one a novel): *The Sun in the Morning* (Faber, 1961), *Earth and Stone* (Faber, 1963), *Sally Cray* (Faber, 1963), *A Place of Stone* (Pantheon, 1964), *The Flame* (Pantheon, 1966), *Walking in the Painted Sunshine* (Faber, 1970), and *Kinship* (Faber, 1973). As they are out of print in the U. S., they have probably failed to attract new readers to his Arthurian novel.

[3] Raymond H. Thompson, "Interviews with Authors of Modern Arthurian Literature: Jim Hunter," from the Camelot Project, University of Rochester, 5/20/89, retrieved at http://www.lib.rochester.edu/Camelot/intrvws/hunter.htm, p. 2.

[4] Norris J. Lacy and Geoffrey Ashe, *The Arthurian Handbook*, (New York: Garland, 1988), pp. 2-5.

[5] "Interviews," p. 2.

[6] Beverly Taylor and Elisabeth Brewer, *The Return of King Arthur: British and American Arthurian Literature Since 1900,* (Cambridge: D.S. Brewer, 1983), p. 310.

[7] Alan Lupak, "'A Very Secondary Position': Perceval in Modern English and American Literature," in *Perceval/Parzival: A Casebook,* eds. Arthur Goos and Norris J. Lacy (New York: Routledge, 2002), pp. 267-86, (275-6).

[8] Hunter, p. 167, cited in Thompson's introduction (ix-xii), p. x.

[9] Iris Murdoch, "The Sovereignty of God and Other Concepts," in *Existentialists and Mystics: Writings on Philosophy and Literature,* ed. and with a preface by Peter Conradi (London: Chatto & Windus, 1997), pp. 363-85.

[10] Søren Kierkegaard, *Fear and Trembling: Repetition,* ed. and trans. Howard V. Hong and Edna H. Hong, (Princeton: Princeton UP, 1983).

[11] Brita K. Stendahl, *Søren Kierkegaard,* (Boston: Twayne, 1976).

[12] Søren Kierkegaard, "Frygt og Bæven," in *Samlede Værker* vol. 5 (Copenhagen: Gyldendal, 1963), pp. 7-111 (63).

[13] See Sidney Johnson, "Doing His Own Thing: Wolfram's Grail," in *A Companion to Wolfram's 'Parzival',* ed. Will Hasty (Columbia: Camden House, 1999), pp. 77-93 (89).

[14] Will Hasty, "At the Limits of Chivalry in Wolfram's *'Parziva'l*: An Arthurian Perspective," in *A Companion to Wolfram's 'Parzival,'* ed. Will Hasty (Columbia: Camden House, 1999), pp. 223-41, (240).

[15] Geoffrey of Monmouth, *History of the Kings of Britain*, trans. Lewis Thorpe, (Harmondsworth: Penguin, 1966), p. 222.

[16] D. H. Green, in *The Art of Recognition in Wolfram's 'Parzival'*, (Cambridge: Cambridge UP, 1982), reminds us of the anonymity of the events at Wolfram's Grail Castle (98), where Amfortas is only mentioned anonymously. In contrast, Hunter's Amfortas figure, Henged, is named when he appears.

[17] 3. Although the adventures of both Chrétien's and Wolfram's heroes take about four and a half years (see Hermann J. Weigand, "Narrative Time in the Grail Poems of Chretien de Troyes and Wolfram von Eshenbach," in *Wolfram's 'Parzival': Five Essays and an* Introduction, ed. Ursula Hoffman, (Ithaca: Cornell UP, 1969), pp. 18-75, (24, 68, 74)), but only two years in Hunter, all three authors give a close account of the early day or days of their hero's adventures and then loosen up the time frame. In fact, Arthur Groos (*Romancing the Grail: Genre, Science, and Quest in Wolfram's 'Parzival'* (Ithaca: Cornell UP, 1995)) calculates Parzival's arrival to Monday, September 29, 1203 at Michaelmass. Significant is the fact that it is not Eastertime when Wolfram's hero first comes to the Grail Castle. It is at Easter the second time, but for Hunter there is no second time as for the two medieval Parcivals Weigand 24, 68, 74), but only two years in Hunter, all three authors give a close account of the early day or days of their hero's adventures and then loosen up the time frame. In fact Arthur Groos calculates Parzival's arrival to Monday, September 29, 1203 at Michaelmass. Significant is the fact that it is not Eastertime when Wolfram's hero first comes to the Grail Castle. It is at Easter the second time, but for Hunter there is no second time as for the two medieval Parcivals

[18] Samuel Taylor Coleridge, "The Rime of the Ancient Mariner," in *Selected Poems*, ed. Richard Holmes (London: HarperCollins, 1996).

[19] T.S. Eliot, "Journey of the Magi," in *Collected Poems, 1909-1962*, (New York: Harcourt, Brace, & World, 1963).

[20] T.S. Eliot, *The Waste Land*, in *Collected Poems, 1909-1962*, (New York: Harcourt, Brace, & World, 1963).

[21] Robert Browning, "Childe Roland to the Dark Tower Came," in *The Poems*, vol. 1, ed. John Pettigrew (New York: Penguin, 1981), pp. 585-92.

[22] *Sir Gawain and the Green Knight: Middle English Text with Facing Translation*, ed. and trans. James Winny (Peterborough: Broadview, 1998)

[23] Chrétien de Troyes, *Perceval: The Story of the Grail*, trans. Nigel Bryant, (Cambridge: D.S. Brewer, 1982).

[24] Chrétien de Troyes, *The Story of the Grail (Li Contes del Graal), or Perceval*, ed. Rupert T. Pickens, trans. William W. Kibler, (New York: Garland, 1990).

[25] Wolfram von Eschenbach, *Parzival*, trans. A.T. Hatto, (London: Penguin, 1980), p. 127.

[26] Justin E. Griffin, *The Holy Grail: The Legend, the History, the Evidence*, (Jefferson: McFarland, 2001), 152.

[27] Ulrich Muller, "Wolfram, Wagner, and the Germans," in *A Companion to Wolfram's 'Parzival'*, ed. Will Hasty, (Columbia: Camden House, 1999), pp. 245-58.

# The Medievalism of Kantorowicz:
## *Bildung,* Jewish Identity, and National Socialism

### Grace Chiu Chan

For the fledgling medievalist, the first reading of Kantorowicz's *Frederick II* represents a conversion experience of sorts. After a steady diet of turgid, heavily-footnoted Germanic scholarship, one at last becomes aware of the enchantment of history via this rhapsody on a theme of Frederick, illuminated by the brilliance of Kantorowicz's hypnotic prose-poetry, metaphysical speculations, and vast and eclectic learning. For a time, we too engage in emperor-worship. We seek all we can find on Frederick, only to be informed by the ironic voice of historical revisionism that his grandeur had more in it of bombast than of substance. Undaunted, we seek out Kantorowicz the scholar through the medium of his later works, though in this quest we are similarly disappointed: for though the monumental erudition of *The Laudes Regiae* and *The King's Two Bodies* awes us in its breadth, we quickly become aware the rhapsodic enthusiasm that gripped us earlier in Kantorowicz's biography of the *Stupor Mundi* is somehow lacking. Still hopeful, we inquire about Kantorowicz the man, asking: Who was he? What was he like? In the latter search, we must inevitably confront the first German edition of *Frederick II,* whose Swastika-bearing cover seems to belie our faint recollection of Kantorowicz's Jewish ancestry, thus presenting us with a contradiction illustrative of a central paradox which suffuses both Kantorowicz's life and writings.

    The historian seeking out the details of Kantorowicz's biography is bound to experience an initial disappointment. Kantorowicz ordered the destruction of his personal papers upon his death—a request executed with a regrettable thoroughness that has left subsequent historiography much room for interpretation. Most recently, a creative reconstruction of Kantorowicz's life is offered by Alain Boureau's unconventional biography, *Kantorowicz: Stories of a Historian*, in which the skeletal details gleaned from the available documents are fleshed out with a speculative resort to the "parallel lives" found in the personal memoirs of Kantorowicz's contemporaries and supplemented by an in-depth examination of Kantorowicz's work. The thesis that Boureau advances is a compelling one, reminiscent (in inverse fashion) of Lyotard's speculations on Heidegger's Nazism. For Boureau, Kantorowicz's life-long self-alienation from the Jewish portion of his German-Jewish identity and his desire to be absorbed into a collective identity in which he could transcend his origins impacted not only the conduct of his life, but also endowed him with the insight with which to perceive the inner dialectic between the historical and the transcendent which pervades his writings on medieval politics, religion, art, and law.

In framing this analysis of Kantorowicz's biography, I would suggest that Boureau's observations could further be enriched by introducing the concept of *Bildung* and its interaction with German-Jewish identity, as detailed in Paul Mendes-Flohr's elegant study, *German Jews: A Dual Identity*. The latter work might well serve as the companion volume to Boureau's biography for its reconstruction of the cultural ethos out of which German-Jewish intellectuals such as Kantorowicz arose, and for its discussion of the internal tensions within their identity which resulted from the clash between the German acculturation of Jews through the pursuit of *Bildung* and the rise of a racialized concept of German identity.

For Mendes-Flohr, the means by which Jews acquired this dual identity lay in their acculturation to the universalistic philosophy of the German Enlightenment, which enjoined upon them the mastery of the canon of German high culture (*Kultur*), while contributing to the development of an ethos known as *Bildung*, which involved the self-cultivation of the intellect and the aesthetic sensibilities.[1]

The mastery of the works of German high culture, such as the literary masterpieces of Goethe, allowed Jews to partially transcend their lack of ethnic Germaness and gain access to a wider German middle-class culture, that valorized *Bildung* as the means to achieving the social prestige accorded to the appearance of refinement and intellectual achievement—qualities Jews manifested through their prominence as patrons and consumers of the arts, and their scholarly achievements. The *Bildung* ethos, proved especially attractive to Jews in that it was characterized in its early stages by an enlightened liberalism and a syncretistic inclusivity that left it open to all who wished to pursue it.[2]

For Mendes-Flohr, the concept of *Bildung* had its origins in classical Graeco-Roman notions of education, which emphasized a process of interior cultivation with a view towards fully perfecting and developing one's humanity—a project whose quasi-religious, and yet secular overtones had a great appeal for educated Jews. The pursuit of *Bildung* included not only the mastery of High German philosophy, but also the cultivation of a political liberalism and aesthetic appreciation that lay particular emphasis on the qualities of grace, harmony, and discipline. Added to this was *Bildung's* drive towards the realization of a code of ethics based on universal truth, as embodied by Kantian moral philosophy, which contributed to the development of an ethos that accorded well with the teachings of the Hebrew Bible.[3]

While the original scope of this s*Bildung*-inspired humanistic education was universal, in the 19th century its range was delimited exclusively to German works of high culture in the effort to promote a sense of German national identity in opposition to the "barbarous" eclecticism which Nietzsche equated with *Bildung's* original drive towards a cosmopolitan cultural syncretism. Through this process, *Bildung*, particularly in the age of German romanticism, was transformed into a search for an originary German racial myth—a betrayal of its original liberal and universalistic ethos. For Jews, this transformation in the concept of *Bildung* set up a marked dichotomy in identity in which they were torn between the cosmopolitanism of the old *Bildung* and the German nationalism of the new.

Moreover, the inner tension between Jewishness and nationalized *Bildung* acculturation created a condition of spiritual bifurcation within the identity of German-Jews, which thinkers such as Martin Buber struggled to overcome both through their injunction that German-Jews strive for a "mastery of the admixture" and in their continued efforts at cultivating the cultural syncretism that made them citizens of the world rather than members of the German nation-state alone. Jewish intellectuals such as Ludwig Strauss and Walter Benjamin recognized within themselves this spiritual bifurcation and debated the possibility of the construction of a German-Jewish Parnassus, or cultural symbiosis predicated on the values of cultural syncretism.[4] The scholar Hermann Cohen believed that a German-Jewish symbiosis had been achieved in actuality, although his opponents argued against him "…for fostering the "delusion" of a German-Jewish symbiosis that proved so tragically dangerous."[5]

Franz Rosenzweig, himself a catalyst of the Jewish Renaissance which occurred in early twentieth-century Germany, criticized Cohen's naivetÈ, noting that while Jews continued in their cultivation of a pan-European culture, they remained oblivious to the fact that *Bildung* was becoming increasingly particularized along the lines of National Socialism. While Cohen reconciled the dual aspects of his identity by attributing an abstract character to Judaism itself, Rosenzweig attempted to restore to Judaism its original particularism, by arguing that a fundamental tension existed in the Jewish soul, whose metaphysical reality exceeded that of the bifurcation between the German and the Jewish. For Rosenzweig, this fundamental bifurcation lay in the inner dialectic between the status of Jews located in absolute ahistorical time by virtue of religion and their historical place as citizens in the mundane world—a tension that was not something to be overcome, but to be lived as the core of Jewish experience. [6] For Rosenzweig, this peculiarity of Jewish identity had to be accepted with full embrace:

> Nestled in metahistorical seclusion, Judaism stands in a critical tension with history and culture. Individual Jews, however, live this tension within themselves, for they are both denizens of the metahistorical

reality of Judaism and participating citizens of the *umwelt*.[7]

If we take Rosenzweig's claim that Judaism corresponds to an absolute and transcendent reality seriously, we might issue to Boureau a mild challenge: perhaps in Kantorowicz's overarching desire to be absorbed into a corporate body, we see an effort, not at overcoming his Jewishness, but at achieving the interior reclamation of the transcendent, non-temporal reality that (according to Rosenzweig) was constitutive of Judaism.

There can be little question, however, of the high degree of conformity between the "profile" Mendes-Flohr constructs of German Jews steeped in *Bildung* and the life of Kantorowicz. Kantorowicz's birthplace, the small town of Poznan, was situated on the border between Germany and Poland and was itself a site of contested identities, at once Polish, Jewish, and Germane-Prussian. The population, though ethnically mixed, underwent a process of forced Germanization following the triumph of the Prussian regime during the 19th century. The Jewish population of Poznan allied itself with the Prussians in the face of anti-Semitic hostility directed at it by the working-class Poles of the town and underwent a thorough German acculturation that carried with it the benefits of citizenship. Politically, Jews of Poznan invariably sided with the Germans in the nationalist conflicts that rent Poznan, as attested by Kantorowicz's own military service against Polish insurgents in 1918. This solidarity with German interests also prevented the growth of Zionism or Socialism among the Jews of Poznan.[8] For Boureau, this climate of German self-identification had made an indelible impression on Kantorowicz: "...his acculturation and assimilation as a German allowed him to ignore the Jewish factor in his life....For Kantorowicz, as for his sisters and cousins, the German University was probably a powerful vehicle for forgetting these ties..."[9]

Like other devotees of *Bildung*, Kantorowicz was the scion of a wealthy bourgeoisie family which owed its material success to the manufacture of liquor—an industry with particular associations with Jewish culture. While the family resources gave Kantorowicz the freedom to pursue his dilettantish and scholarly interests, Boureau discerns in Kantorowicz's life an obsession with escaping from the social opprobrium attached to both his family's Jewishness and its links to manufacturing. Like other German-Jews who adopted *Bildung*, Kantorowicz may have found in it a means of acquiring a kind of pseudo-aristocratic patent of respectability.

Kantorowicz's intellectual pedigree, however, was utterly beyond reproach. Again, his dazzling and wide-ranging scholarship was a product of the culture of *Bildung* in which he was steeped. The fact that other members of his family became prominent academics, such as his cousin Gertrud, an art historian, and his cousin Richard, a distinguished anthropologist, speaks to the learned

German-Jewish milieu of which he was a product—a phenomenon in keeping with the observation that cultivated German-Jews displayed a striking degree of overrepresentation at German Universities.[10] As Mendes-Flohr observes of Prussia itself: "During the last decade of the 19th century for every 100,000 males of each [religious denomination] in Prussia, there studied in Prussian universities 33 Catholics, 58 Protestants, and 519 Jews."[11]

Kantorowicz's education itself offers us a classic example of *Bildung* acculturation with its emphasis on cultural syncretism. According to the literary scholar Yakov Malkiel, "Ernst attended an excellent humanistic or classical secondary school, the Kaiserin Augusta-Viktoria Gymnasium which offered an exacting nine year curriculum emphasizing such subjects as Greek, Latin, and history …upon entering the Berlin University [Kantorowicz]…could afford to experiment for a while with diverse subjects …"[12] The wide range of Kantorowicz's early education was further enriched by his tour of duty in the Ottoman empire, which prompted him to produce a Ph.D. dissertation on Muslim economics during a further course of study at the University of Munich.

However, the most significant intellectual influence for Kantorowicz would come only when he reached the University of Heidelberg in 1919, where he would fall under the sway of the poet/intellectual, Stefan George. The motivating force behind Kantorowicz's journey to Heidelberg lay in the presence there of two eminent medievalists, Karl Hampe and Frederick Baeghethen—a combination that had also attracted the future Nazi collaborator Percy Schramm, who would, ironically become Kantorowicz's lifelong friend. Kantorowicz's integration into the George circle was facilitated by the connections he possessed through his learned German-Jewish intellectual milieu—in this case, introductions provided to him by his sister Elizabeth, wife of the intellectual Arthur Salz, who had entertained George in her Heidelberg home on many occasions, and his cousin Gertrud, who was a personal friend of George. During Kantorowicz's membership in George's exclusive "salon," while he continued his intellectual diversification with forays into ancient history and Renaissance art, it was ultimately George's medievalism which would prove decisive in Kantorowicz's career as a historian.[13]

Stefan George, a German Romantic poet turned symbolist, was himself a devotee of the early concept of *Bildung* on the Goethean model in that "[h]e sought to free the masses from decadence by preaching a doctrine of universal beauty adapted to ethics, daily life, and language."[14] Like Heidegger, George was interested in redeeming the corroding effects of modernity, through the creation of a group of hyper-educated intellectual supermen who were to preach the George gospel by their co-optation of academic chairs at leading German universities. In this effort, George published a literary journal entitled

*The Yearbook* and held regular symposia, at which his intimates addressed him as "Meister".[15] It was in 1919 that Kantorowicz fell under the spell of the "poet-guru," who had involved his disciples in the worship of the medieval Emperor Frederick II, upon whose tomb Kantorowicz and other George pupils laid a wreath in commemoration of the 700th anniversary of the emperor's founding of the University of Naples. The lionization of Frederick among the George disciples was an offshoot of their obsession with the revival of what they termed the "Hidden Germany." Despite its nationalist resonances, the George circle's "Hidden Germany" was more a metaphysical concept than a politically realizable entity that involved a striving for the renewal of the German spirit through the semi-mythical recreations of poets and writers, whose ranks Kantorowicz was soon to join.

Despite the friendship of George with prominent German-Jewish intellectuals such as Kantorowicz, there are some suggestions that George viewed the Jewish members of his circle with ambivalence. As Mendes-Flohr notes, George, while recognizing the Jewish capacity to master the national canon, continued to cling to the idea of some fundamental racial difference, suggesting that Jews did not feel as deeply as Germans did, and vowing that "I will never allow them to become the majority in my Society or *Yearbook*."[16] An awareness of the position taken by Kantorowicz's old master on his Jewish disciples poses for us again the question of what attitude Kantorowicz himself took towards the Jewish portion of his identity. Evidence exists that Kantorowicz experienced anti-Semitism first hand within the ranks of the George circle in that one of its members, Baron Uxhull (to whom *Frederick II* was dedicated), suggested that Kantorowicz be barred from giving public lectures lest the George clique be associated with Jews. Boureau suggests that Kantorowicz's Jewishness was never allowed to be forgotten, even among the members of learned society, recounting an incident where Kantorowicz's earlier mentor in ancient history suggested that his pupil take up Jewish or Oriental studies as more "acceptable" alternative to his pupil's planned concentration in western civilization.[17] While Boureau suggests a fundamental atheism in Kantorowicz's personal orientation to religion, the medievalist Norman F. Cantor argues for a more complete polarization within Kantorowicz's personality in this essay "The Nazi Twins," claiming on the one hand that "Kantorowicz's Nazi credentials were impeccable on every count in except his race," [18] while also insisting that "Kantorowicz thought of himself as Jew and hated the Catholic Church. Once a year at Passover, he was moved to comment on this particular holiday of freedom and what it meant to him…"[19] Despite these conflicting views, Malkiel's assessment of Kantorowicz's sense of Jewish identity seems to echo Mendes-Flohr's concept of *Bildung* in his assertion that "[t]hough Kantorowicz's Judaism was far more subdued and residual than...Gundolf's...it breaks through in his intense intellectualism, in the cosmopolitan sweep of his curiosity..."[20] Malkiel reinforces this element of Judaism in Kantorowicz's identity in his statement that the later possessed "intellectualized religion...[and a] steady concern with spiritual traditions... in his inquiries into theocracy."[21]

Despite the reservations of the "the master," the George circle was itself an instantiation of internal bifurcation, divided as it was between its German-Jewish members and its conservative German and rabidly nationalistic followers. As Yakov Malkiel remarks, "the paradox has often been tangentially mentioned...that no less than one half of George's immediate followers...were...either Jews...or of partially Jewish ancestry...the ranks of the poet's Gentile friends included several mild, and a few violent, irate, anti-Semites...George himself [is]...best classed as a neo-Pagan...[who] undeniably felt attracted to Jewish men and ...to Jewish women."[22]

There can be little doubt that the culture of *Bildung* made the creation of this strange meeting ground possible. Malkiel suggests that the Jewish attraction to the circle becomes explicable in light of the fact that its Jewish members were drawn from the most acculturated members of the German-Jewish population, who (like Kantorowicz) deeply identified with the German element of their identity, and scorned what they perceived as the vulgar, materialistic socialism which they associated with liberal politics, in favor of the aristocratic conservatism promulgated by the Georgians, which, together with their reactionary predilection for ancient and medieval civilization, set them in opposition with the current atmosphere of German politics. Kantorowicz's own military service provides evidence of his predisposition toward political conservatism. The crisis of World War I and the patriotic service of Jews in the German army brought with it a misplaced hope that their wartime demonstrations of loyalty to the national cause would guarantee them full inclusion in the life of the nation-state.[23] Kantorowicz, too, served his country patriotically in World War I, where he earned the iron cross second-class for valor, and later fought against the Poles together with the Prussians for control of Poznan. Later, in January 1919, he helped quell the Spartacist uprising in Berlin. In each instance, Kantorowicz displayed an exemplary political conservatism.[24]

Similarly, Cantor sees in Kantorowicz (and his "Nazi Twin," Schramm) evidence of a conservative reaction to the dual threat of communism and the vulgarity of the Weimar Republic, and the post-war fragmentation and economic decline of Germany, for which the restitution of the Hohenstaufen Empire might serve as a panacea. For Cantor, Kantorowicz's writing and his reactionary bias towards the Middle Ages arose from the tradition of German idealism, which seems roughly equivalent to the *Bildung* ethos reconstructed by Mendes-Flohr.²⁵

Boureau also highlights traces of this conservatism in Kantorowicz in that "[b]y obstinately pursuing his reactionary trajectory Kantorowicz was able to discern governmental forms and procedures that would have escaped a more innocent person. The suspicion remains and gives rise to another, simpler narrative that of the life of a young man from the Prussian bourgeoisie that only his status as a Jew removed, despite his own wishes, from a conservative vocation."²⁶

It was in the service of this political conservatism and at the instigation of George that Kantorowicz produced his monumental biography to Frederick II, in the hopes of inspiring the German people to new greatness. For Kantorowicz, the creation of *Frederick II* was a five-year process which was not completed until 1927. The biography received wild popular acclaim upon its appearance, exhausting a first edition of 10,000 copies within two years. The future Nazi bigwig Hermann Goring was said to have admired both the book and Kantorowicz. However, the German academic establishment regarded such popular success for a putatively "historical" work with a predictable skepticism. The mediaevalist Albert Brackmann led the critics, belittling *Frederick II* as a mere mythicization, noting the absence of footnotes and bibliography in the original edition. Kantorowicz's riposte was a 500-page companion volume to Frederick II, consisting entirely of critical apparatus that silenced his detractors. It was on the basis of *Frederick II* that Kantorowicz bargained for and obtained an honorary professorship at the University of Frankfurt—a post made official in 1932, when Kantorowicz was awarded a chair of medieval history upon the death of its occupant. Kantorowicz's temporary integration into an institution of higher learning was not to last however, as Hitler's star climbed steadily. The fragile rapprochement created within the ranks of the George circle between Germans and German Jews was to be shattered by the coming of Nazism. While Master George himself accepted honors from the new regime and took pleasure in the realization (at least in part) for his project of a revived Germany, he later withdrew into indignant retirement in Switzerland, after his sister was asked to provide proof of her purity of German descent. The anti-Semitic remnants of the George circle made a travesty of the Master's work by distorting its Nationalism into a kind of proto-Nazi propaganda, issuing publications of their work inscribed with appalling dedications to both George and the Fuehrer.²⁷

While Kantorowicz remained loyal to the memory of the master, serving as one of the pall-bearers at his funeral, he too, would shortly become a victim of Nazi fanaticism. In 1933, all Jews, save veterans, were barred from positions of authority, including university professorships. Kantorowicz, feeling the effects of this climate, attempted a belated rehabilitation of his *Frederick II* in a 1933 lecture, where he emphasized the benign Nationalism of the medieval emperor, setting it in contrast to the pernicious racism of the Nazis.[28] The damage, however, had already been done. Fearing expulsion from Frankfurt (though a veteran himself), Kantorowicz pre-empted the administration by resigning his post in a letter that reveals his deep sense of betrayal, which Boureau reproduces in part:

> I never dreamed—I , who volunteered for military service in 1914, I , who fought during, and , again after the war against the Poles in Poznan, against the Spartacist insurrection in Berlin, and against the Republic of the Councils in Munich—I never thought that I could expect to be stripped of my post because of my Jewish ancestry. It seemed to me that thanks to my writings on the Emperor Frederick II Hohenstaufen, I would not need proof, either past or present of my feelings in favor of a Germany re-oriented towards nationalism. It appeared to me that my fundamental enthusiasm for a nationalist state went well beyond the ordinary feeling (so readily swayed by events), nor has it been eroded by current affairs…However, for myself, as a Jew, I am forced to draw clear conclusions as regards what is going on and to put aside my professional duties for the spring semester.[29]

For Boureau, this letter reveals Kantorowicz's "rude awakening" and "betrays more dismay that a pleasant dream has been interrupted than indignation in the face of this anti-Semitic ignominy."[30] Yet this passage seems to afford us yet another poignant illustration of Mendes-Flohr's reconstruction of the spiritual bifurcation of the German-Jew manifested in this expression of Kantorowicz's "double-self-consciousness," as Kantorowicz, the patriotic German-nationalist who views his Jewishness as a distant and vitiated "ancestry," is brought into a present-tense confrontation by the Nazis with "…myself as a Jew." Furthermore, Kantorowicz's remark that his "enthusiasm for the nationalist state…has not been eroded by present events" must strike us as bizarre, but here again, Mendes-Flohr's analysis proves instructive when we recognize that Kantorowicz's conception of German nationalism as idiosyncratically "Jewish," predicated on the *Bildung* promoted by the German Enlightenment, and embodied in the medieval figure of Frederick II, which Kantorowicz identified not with the irrational, racialized nationalism of the Nazis, but with the devotion to pan-European culture that Franz Rosenzwig characterized as the German-Jew's peculiar definition of *Deutschtum*. In Kantorowicz's continued adherence to this notion of *Bildung* qua nationalism, even at a moment of severe personal and historical crisis, we see his blindness both to its obsolescence and to the isolation of the position in which it had enmeshed him.

Later in life, in the essay collection significantly entitled *Pro Patria Mori*, Kantorowicz appears to reveal a full consciousness of how tragically his monumental history of Frederick II had been misinterpreted in the cause of the racist Nazi re-mythicization of the German people in his comment that: "We will leave to the reader the job of identifying the many distortions that the concept of *corpus mysticum* has undergone, thanks to appropriations by nationalist, racist, and political doctrines both in former times and in recent years...nationalist aberrations that odiously distort a venerable and originally high-minded concept." [31] But in 1933, Kantorowicz had not yet reached the fullness of this awareness, evading the official resignation he had threatened by utilizing the connections to the German nobility that he had forged during his membership in the George coterie. Even after the Nazi leadership imposed a loyalty oath on faculty in 1934 and his own classroom was disturbed by Nazi protesters, Kantorowicz's solution was not flight, but a withdrawal into emeritus status, in an effort to avoid the obligation to take the fascist vow.[32] However, the violent events of *Kristallnacht* at last forced Kantorowicz to embark on his own personal Diaspora. Tragically, Kantorowicz's mother and sister chose to remain behind and would later perish in concentration camps.[33]

After his flight from Germany, the story of Kantorowicz's life becomes a tale of scholarly wanderings that brought him variously to Oxford, Berkeley, and ultimately Princeton. It was at Berkeley that Kantorowicz would experience an eerie repeat of the Nazi incident of 1934. In 1949, the United States was involved in a wave of anti-Communist paranoia brought on by the "Red" hunts led by Senator Joseph McCarthy. Officials at Berkeley began to require an anti-Communist loyalty oath of its faculty, which Kantorowicz had recently joined as a professor of medieval English history. Kantorowicz refused on the grounds that: "It is an inoffensive oath to begin with....before producing those changes that little by little will render it less inoffensive: Italy under Mussolini in 1931, the Germany of Hitler in 1933 offered terrifying and clear examples of the inoffensive and gradual process by which political oaths were imposed."[34] In his ideal of the university, Kantorowicz recognized the institutional expression of the cult of *Bildung*—an ideal violated time and time again by the imposition of fascist oaths, first by the Nazis and then by the communists.[35] After a brief struggle with the administration, Kantorowicz resigned, though in 1951 he quickly found a berth at Princeton's Institute for Advanced Study, through the influence of his friends Robert Oppenheimer and the German-Jewish ÈmigrÈ, Erwin Panofsky. It was in Princeton that Kantorowicz was to finish out both his life and career, devoting himself to the composition of his magnum opus, *The King's Two Bodies*— a task that would absorb him till his death in 1963.[36]

Where these biographical traces leave off, the story of Kantorowicz's works begin. An examination of Kantorowicz's three major contributions to medieval scholarship, *Frederick II*, *Laudes Regiae*, and *The King's Two Bodies*, in addition to providing instantiations of Kantorowicz's German, Berkeley, and Princeton phases, allows us to discern his intellectual evolution away from his youthful devotion to nationalist *Bildung* to his final exploration of the dualisms of identity found in the *King's Two Bodies*. In all his works, however, the tension between nationalism and Jewishness is already present in both implicit and explicit forms. Again, for Boureau, the political insights on the evolution of the state which Kantorowicz enshrined in *The King's Two Bodies* were intimately connected to his own fantasy of transcending his identity as the heir to a Jewish manufacturing dynasty: "For the moment it is enough to note that fatherland for which Kantorowicz fought was less Germany, as such, than 'a state.' It was an empty space on which to project his desire to escape from the circuit of a wine salesman."[37] However, even earlier than this, the internal tensions within Kantorowicz can be reconstructed through the reading of *Frederick II*. *Frederick II* was Kantorowicz's homage to the "Hidden Germany" of the George circle, appearing with the swastika/rising sun insignia with which George stamped his *Yearbook*. That was only the beginning of the misunderstanding. The message of *Frederick II* was both distorted and misconstrued, while its final lines, imbued with nationalistic fervor, were twisted into the prediction of the coming of a new Fuhrer—an utter perversion of Kantorowicz's highly personal nationalistic message which retained within it the syncretism and pluralism of *Bildung*.

Again, Kantorowicz composed *Frederick II* in the 1920s, at a time when German National identity had splintered into factions, among which National Socialism was one of many competing parties. In Frederick II, Kantorowicz perceived a figure who embodied a German identity that was capable of transcending such fragmentation by combining contradictions into a syncretistic whole, or, as Alain Boureau phrases it, "Kantorowicz saw in this 13$^{th}$ century emperor—as Latin as he was Germanic, as learned as he was powerful, administrator as well as visionary—the ferment of a German identity on the rise, superior to the divisions and inertia of the present."[38]

Later in life, and stung by the misappropriations of his youthful work, Kantorowicz refused to license a second edition, as "[t]he book was inspired by an enthusiasm peculiar to the 1920s, rife with its hopes for the triumph of a secret Germany and for the renewal of the German people by contemplating their greatest emperor. The book is now out of date and runs the risk of encouraging an outmoded nationalism."[39]

Within this account of a German national hero, traces of Kantorowicz's Jewish self-reflexivity appear, clearly inflected by influence of *Bildung*. It is apparent from the outset that the whole biography is a celebration of Kantorowicz's own ethos, with Frederick refashioned as the spiritual and intellectual twin of George and of Kantorowicz himself. Kantorowicz's devotion to cultural syncretism is apparent in the lines where he hymns Palermo, the island of Frederick's youth, as a kind of bastion of multiculturalism where "religions and customs jostled each other before his eyes: mosques with their minarets, synagogues with their cupolas stood cheek by jowl with Norman churches...adorned by Byzantine masters."[40] Here, Frederick the autodidact, like Kantorowicz and other adherents of *Bildung*, cultivates in himself the knowledge classics, mastering Latin, Arabic and Greek in addition to his native Sicilian and German. The invidious contrast Kantorowicz sets up between Otto the Welf (Frederick's rival for the imperial crown), whom he caricatures as an Aryan strong man with "—an amazing lack of education, a poverty of intellect...heroic foolhardiness...unwontedly tall...his strength lay in his might fist..."[41], and the figure of the brilliantly cosmopolitan Frederick reflects Kantorowicz's own sense of Germanness not as the product of racial myth, but as the creation of the *Bildung*-style culture which Kantorowicz associates with Frederick who "exploited not German peculiarities, but German world forces....It was not common German traditions which bound the Northerners together, but Roman form and culture..."[42] In other words, the universalistic syncretism of the Empire.

Kantorowicz's self-reflexivity also appears in his discussion of Frederick's treatment of his Jewish subjects, whom he set apart, ordering them to mark their clothes with a patch and to wear their beards long. Kantorowicz remarks that such measures formed part of the emperor's need to demarcate the boundaries of his kingdom, but makes no further comment. Later on, however, Kantorowicz suggests that the worship of the person of Frederick himself was to form a cult that transcended the particularism of religious identity in that the emperor's birthday was proclaimed a holiday to be observed by all denominations of the empire.[43] Most interesting for our present study is Kantorowicz's discussion of the Emperor's policy towards the treatment of the Jews, recorded in the Constitutions of Melfi. Malkiel attributes Kantorowicz's foregrounding of Frederick's policy towards his Jewish and Muslim subjects as a "strongly assimilated but not entirely enucleated, German Jew in the youthful historian."[44]

Kantorowicz himself observed that the measures of toleration in the Melfian document were of a limited sort. Again, the Jews of Sicily were obliged to mark themselves with distinctive dress and appearance and subject to harsh penalty if they violated these directives. Kantorowicz notes that, "[f]or the rest the Jews were permitted, nay obliged, to live according to their own laws."[45]

Moreover, under Frederick, Jews were free of anti-usury laws and protected against the harassment of the Church and accusations of ritual murder. Kantorowicz praises Frederick for his rigorous examination and dismissal of a case of ritual murder brought against the Jews of Fulda,[46] and for his statement that "no innocent man shall be oppressed because he is a Jew or a Saracen."[47] It also interesting to note that Kantorowicz draws attention to Frederick's interest in Jewish philosophy through contacts with Hebrew thinkers, crediting the emperor himself with the knowledge of Hebrew. Frederick's court is itself portrayed as a Stefan George-like circle of intellectuals and poets among whom Jewish philosophers were prominent, among them Juda Ben Salomon Levi, a translator of Greek philosophy, and Jacob ben Abbamari, a specialist in Arabic and Aristotelian philosophy. These Jewish thinkers and scholars prepared Hebrew translations of key philosophical texts that were dedicated to the Emperor with the wish that the Messiah would return during his reign. According to Kantorowicz, Maimonides was a frequent subject of conversation[48] in this charmed circle, where "knightly and aristocratic officials...mixed with and argued with Christian, Jewish, and Muslim philosophers."[49] Also significant is Kantorowicz's characterization of Frederick as a man of dual identity—a union of opposites, as "Fredericus Cornutus, [whose]... two horns are the token of the Messiah, symbols not of evil but of power as Moses shows and Alexander..."[50] Within the text of *Frederick II*, Kantorowicz explicitly disowned the idea of the hegemony of racial Germans:

> The domination of one race over the others would have been a betrayal in one peculiar type for in the state dominated by one race...the best powers of all the races could never flourish equally, to produce one world-embracing...no single race possessed a world sense...the feeling for the universal...incorporate only in the super-national German whole. Frederick never contemplated such a betrayal. He was...no German king, he was solely Roman Caesar and Imperator...centering in himself and his own person the German whole...which supplied the one possible form of the self-fulfillment Germany was then seeking: self-fulfillment within the Roman Empire.[51]

Thus, in this apostrophe to Frederick, we find Kantorowicz's highest paean to the universalizing, syncretistic ethos of *Bildung*, which he, as a German Jew had thoroughly absorbed. For Robert Lerner, the Frederick II whom Kantorowicz lionized was not a racist proto-Fuhrer, but rather a cosmopolitan Renaissance man before his time, "a dynastic hybrid, half-German, half-Norman, who wished to bring to Germany gifts from the Mediterranean World, such as classical learning."[52] In this apt characterization of Kantorowicz's panegyric to the emperor, it is an irresistible temptation to see not merely the apotheosis of a medieval figure, but a valorization of Kantorowicz's own ethos and personality, which might easily explain his predisposition to Frederick. But, sadly, rabid German Nationalists, incapable of grasping such subtleties, seized only upon Kantorowicz's closing lament that "[t]he greatest Frederick is not yet redeemed, him his people knew not and sufficed not. 'Lives and lives not.' The Sibyl's word is not for the Emperor, but for the German people,"[53] as a prophecy of the rise of Hitler and the Nazi party.

The *Laudes Regiae* represents the middle period of Kantorowicz's scholarship, coinciding with the phase of his life that followed his expulsion from Frankfurt and preceded the loyalty oath controversy at Berkeley. The monograph represents Kantorowicz's effort to trace the tortuous lineage of the motto "Christus Vincit, Regnat, et Imperat" back to its Romano-Frankish origins. In contrast to *Frederick II*, *The Laudes* is a dry model of hyper-detailed scholarship that loses itself in its own erudition. Moreover, it is, unlike *Frederick II*, a work of de-mythicization—the reduction of a magical, apotropaeic motto, to a mere linguistic hybrid of Roman imperial slogans given a Christianizing patina by the Franks. It is in this deconstruction of the propagandistic mantras of imperial power that Kantorowicz offers us an oblique insight into the confrontation with his Jewish identity. Now, rather than serving as the mythicizer of power and tyranny, Kantorowicz takes on the task of debunker. The formula examined in *The Laudes* serves Kantorowicz as the jumping-off point for a number of incisive observations on the mechanisms that govern the creation of an imperial cult of personality and the sacralization of a lay ruler. Following the traces of the "Vincit" formula, Kantorowicz uncovers a series of Frankish lauds wherein the Emperor assigns to himself Christ-like qualities through an appropriation of the "Christus formula," at the expense of the Pope who can claim only the second spiritual place. As Kantorowicz notes, these transcendentalizing acclamations were sung as part of a whole complex of imperial propaganda that surrounded imperial crowning and feast days. Moreover, the Romanized form of this acclamation appears in combination with the names of the kings of the Old Testament—a peculiarity that points Kantorowicz to another observation that might have been inflected by his German-Jewish identity. For, as he observes, the Carolingians, rather than appropriating the Roman style of rulership, re-created themselves along the lines of Hebrew Old Testament rulers: "The model which was consciously followed, in the eighth century at least, was the image of the kings of the Old Testament, anointed chieftains of a tribe like the early Carolingians...the antimony between the *Regnum Davidicum* and *Imperium Romanum* was deep-rooted...But ever since 800, the older and more powerful image of Christus-imperator interfered with Frankish conception of a Davidic priest-kingship."[54]

Here, we find both a recognition of the "Judaizing" quality of early Frankish kingship, as well as an appreciation of its uneasy co-existence with Roman concepts of rulership—insights which may reflect the dualism of Kantorowicz's own personality.[55] Evidence of Kantorowicz's new efforts at making a critical inquiry into the mechanisms of power is revealed by his concluding remarks in the *Laudes*, where he notes:

> Political acclamations have been resuscitated systematically in the authoritarian countries. They are indispensable to the emotionalism of a Fascist Regime...full scope to meditation was given...to... [the]...historian... on the dangers implicit in his profession of excavator of the past –when he heard the Italian Balillas sing:
> Christis vincit, Christis regnat, Christus imperat!
> ...
> Duci Benito Mussolini Italicae gentis gloriae, pax, vita
> Et salus perpetua![56]

The unified grandeur of the emperors like Frederick which Kantorowicz demystifies with the critical gaze of the *Laudes* ultimately fractures into the dichotomies explored in the culmination of his scholarship, *The King's Two Bodies*—which is in and of itself a study of dual identity: "...the *persona mixta*, the mixed person...the yoking together of the seemingly heterogeneous spheres had a peculiar attraction for an age eager to reconcile the duality of this world and the other..."[57]

In this passage, however, Kantorowicz is speaking not of the dual identity of German-Jews, but the late medieval development of a dualistic political theology of kingship, developed by royal jurists in their effort to transcendentalize the medieval ruler by positing for him the existence of two bodies—a "body corporal," represented by the physical body of the individual occupant of the throne, and a "body mystical," represented by the regal office which persisted even beyond the decay of the fleshly body, and thus serving to preserve the continuity of kingship beyond the death of each individual monarch. In constructing this ideal, medieval legalists drew upon ecclesiastical language and the idea of the mystical body of the church to create this sacralizing mystique for the person of the ruler. In examining Kantorowicz's reconstruction of this medieval political concept, one wonders to what degree Kantorowicz's consciousness of his own duality as German-Jew shaped his capacity to perceive the dualisms operating in this theology. For Boureau, the connection is unmistakable:

> Collective identity does go without saying: it eludes the individual, just as it endlessly escaped Kantorowicz...[he]...had sought to ground his identity....this second perpetual, immanent body...in the Prussian

fatherland...and finally in the University from 1930 to 1949....The course of his biography...makes it possible to understand his obsession with a double ontological status...In Kantorowicz's writing, the conception of a double body...membership in the second body could be found beyond the statist form taken at the end of the Middle Ages, in the condition of mankind, that humanitas whose definition of Kantorowicz discerned in Dante, who had become for him an object of unfailing admiration such as he had not experienced since writing Frederick II...Kantorowicz's biographical trajectory turns him into an analogue of medieval man, who had passed from the immense solitude of the feudal...to an elaboration of humanism with Dante.[58]

Despite this perception, Kantorowicz's thought seems to come full circle in *The King's Two Bodies*, which seems not so much an injunction towards assimilation into the collective identity of the University as a revalorization of *Bildung* in the form of the principle of Universalism as means of transcending earthly dichotomies embodied in the thought of Dante, who suggested that the "body" of humankind be subjected to the guiding and ultimately salvific intelligence of a single Roman emperor on the model of Frederick II.[59] Thus, in the closing chapter of The *King's Two Bodies*, which is both a survey and a muted celebration of Dante's *De Monarchia,* we see the circularity of Kantorowicz's own thought in his return to the universalizing tendencies of *Bildung* qua salvation, extended beyond the boundaries of the German nation state to embrace the whole of humanity.

With this we, too, might return to the examination of Kantorowicz's life. Did it come full circle as well? Or did he succeed in achieving a "mastery of the admixture" in his own identity along the lines of Mendes-Flohr? In Kantorowicz's written protest against the imposition of the loyalty oath, we clearly perceive far more self-awareness than that with which Boureau credits him: "I know by joining the white Battalions I have prepared, if indirectly and against my intention, the road leading to National-Socialism and its rise to power."[60] While for Boureau, the "biographical trajectory" to be reconstructed from a survey of Kantorowicz's major work consists of variations on the theme of "double-ontological status" and the search for a communal identity in which Kantorowicz could transcend his own Jewishness, Robert Lerner discerns in the intellectual movement from *Frederick II* to *The King's Two Bodies* a definite note of penitence, a renunciation of the uncritical and irrational use of history as Nietzschean monument or as Heideggerean myth in favor of the objective, heavily erudite productions of the historical scholar: "his writings contain scattered critical references to 'Fascist devotions,' 'nationalistic ravings,'....Determined himself to avoid 'ravings,' he altered his style...he now meant to subvert 'devotions'...by dissecting them clinically."[61]

To expand on Lerner's statement, we may perceive in Kantorowicz's later works an increase in self-critical awareness that mirrors their author's movement away from his earlier role as the rhapsode of the Emperor (and by extension the Nazi regime), enthralled by the Svengaliesque charisma of Stefan George, to his gradual transformation into the detached historical scholar who seeks to deconstruct and critique the mechanisms by which charisma exerts itself both in the form of slogan/ritual (*Laudes*) and ideology/rhetoric (*The King's Two Bodies*). Kantorowicz seems, in the latter stages of his career, concerned with unmasking the power of which he earlier found himself the unwitting dupe.

As for the outcome of Kantorowicz's inner struggle, Malkiel's insights on Kantorowicz's personality provide a pithy summation: "His problem was, from the start, to reconcile certain conflicting strains in himself, and the difficulty grew more acute as new and unforeseen experiences increased the number of elements that had to balance against one another."[62] Arguably, however, the resolution of this tension in Kantorowicz's own life posed a paradox as indissoluble as the dualisms which permeate The *King's Two Bodies*. If we may depart for a moment from the rigors of the historian and adopt Boureau's technique of imaginative reconstruction, we might see in Kantorowicz's destruction of his own biographical traces and effort to cut the Gordian knot of this spiritual bifurcation. For by annihilating the body corporal of his own historical personality, perhaps Kantorowicz sought to leave only the unity formed by the mystical corpus of his scholarship, of which it may truly be said:

"Dignitas non moritur."

*UNIVERSITY OF ILLINOIS—URBANA*

NOTES

[1] Paul Mendes-Flohr, *German Jews: A Dual Identity*, (New Haven: Yale UP, 1999), p. 3.
[2] Ibid. pp. 9-10.
[3] Ibid. pp10, 27-9.
[4] Ibid. pp. 40-59.
[5] Ibid. p. 60.
[6] Ibid. pp. 78-84.
[7] Ibid. p.83.
[8] Alain Boureau, *Kantorowicz: Stories of a Historian*. (Baltimore: John Hopkins UP, 1990), pp. 57-66.
[9] Ibid. p.67.
[10] Ibid. p. 30-4.

[11] Ibid. p. 33.
[12] Yakov Malkiel, "Ernst H. Kantorowicz," in *On Four Modern Humanists: Hofmannstahl, Gundolf, Curtius, Kantorowicz*. (Princeton: Princeton UP, 1970), p. 55.
[13] Ibid. pp.155, 160.
[14] Ibid. p. 19.
[15] Malkiel, pp. 23, 170-4.
[16] Mendes-Flohr, p. 19.
[17] Boureau, p. 66.
[18] Norman F. Cantor, Inventing the Middle Ages. (New York: William Morrow and Company, 1991), p. 95.
[19] Ibid. p. 80.
[20] Malkiel, p. 199.
[21] Ibid. p. 215.
[22] Malkiel, p. 179.
[23] Mendes-Flohr, p. 20.
[24] Boureau, p. 30.
[25] Cantor, pp. 104, 112-117.
[26] Boureau, p. 106.
[27] Malkiel, p. 180.
[28] Robert E. Lerner, "Ernst H. Kantorowicz," in *Medieval Scholarship: Biographical Studies in the Formation of a Discipline*, vol. 1 (New York: Garland, 1995), p. 267.
[29] Boureau, p. 12.
[30] Ibid. p. 12.
[31] Ibid. p. 43.
[32] Ibid. pp. 78-80.
[33] Malkiel, p. 200.
[34] Boureau, p. 84.
[35] Ibid. pp. 63-7.
[36] Cantor, p. 101.
[37] Boureau, p. 55.
[38] Ibid. p. 12.
[39] Ibid. p. 13.
[40] Ernst H. Kantorowicz, *Frederick I* (London: Constable & Co., 1931), pp. 1-50.
[41] Ibid. p 65.
[42] Ibid. 79.
[43] Ibid. pp. 121, 227.
[44] Malkiel, p. 184.
[45] Kantorowicz, p. 268.
[46] Ibid. p. 413.
[47] Ibid. 269.
[48] Ibid. 344-5, 415.
[49] Ibid. p. 346.
[50] Ibid. p. 609.
[51] Ibid. p. 385.

[52] Lerner, p. 266.
[53] *Frederick II*, p. 687.
[54] Ernst H. Kantorowicz, *Laudes Regiae*, (Berkeley: U of California P, 1958), pp. 62-3.
[55] Ibid., pp. 62-3.
[56] Ibid. pp. 185-6.
[57] Ernst H. Kantorowicz, *The King's Two Bodies*, (Princeton: Princeton UP, 1960), p. 43.
[58] Boureau, p. 99-100.
[59] *The King's Two Bodies*, p. 472.
[60] Lerner, p. 268.
[61] Ibid. p. 271.
[62] Malkiel, p. 218.

# Reigning Arthur In:
## Mythological Appropriation and the English Monarchy

Marjon Ames

In the 12th century, Geoffrey of Monmouth described the legendary King Arthur as:

> ... a young man only fifteen years old; but he was of outstanding courage and generosity, and his inborn goodness gave him such grace that he was loved by almost all the people ... In Arthur courage was closely linked with generosity ... The justness of his cause encouraged him, for he had a claim by rightful inheritance to the kingship of the whole island.[1]

Few rulers ever receive the high praise that Geoffrey of Monmouth gave King Arthur. His reign set the figurative standard for medieval English kings, who adopted Arthurian mythology to increase their power in a variety of ways. This is not an examination of the historical Arthur; rather, it is an attempt to determine how later medieval English kings used these early medieval legends to strengthen and, at times, legitimize themselves, as was necessitated by the constant political upheaval of the fifteenth century.[2] Arthur's significance to the people increased as the English conquered more of Wales under Edward I, beginning in 1277. The Welsh kept and disseminated many of the legends of the historical king. Arthur was supposed to have descended from Constantine, as well as Brutus and Aeneas, and was thus linked to the most ancient and powerful ruling tradition in Britain. He later became a national hero who was prophesied to return one day as the rightful king of all of Britain. When English kings expressed interest in Arthur, the Welsh grew in importance. Furthermore, Arthur became the Welsh hope for liberation from English rule. A. D. Carr writes: "The story of their Trojan descent gave them a link with the world of classical antiquity, especially Rome, since Brutus was said to have been a descendant of Aeneas."[3] Arthur enabled them to link themselves, via their Romano-British predecessors, to the wealth of Trojan and Roman myth.

The Welsh claimed Arthur as an important figure in their heritage, and those English kings who dealt significantly with the Welsh worked the hardest to align themselves with him. English kings believed that they needed to ground their authority in the hopes of the people they conquered. They needed the economic and military strength and respect of these least likely supporters and the legitimacy that only a connection to someone like Arthur could provide. Furthermore, English kings, who held questionable claims to the English throne and the associated dominion over Wales, were especially intrigued by the legend of Arthur's anticipated but improbable return to the throne. James Merriman states: "Arthur succeeds to the throne despite his clouded title...abroad he extends his conquests, and at home maintains a court to which come the greatest knights of the world to live in gallantry and honor under his liberal reign."[4] By establishing themselves as Arthur's successors, medieval English kings were able to fulfill the prophecy of Arthur's fabled return by proxy. This effort discouraged the likelihood of insurgence among the people, since their rightful king was in power. To wit, the self-identification of particular English kings to the figure of King Arthur amounted cumulatively to the identification of English kingship with the future king. Edward I initiated this practice, and subsequent English kings used it to greater and lesser degrees.

Regardless of the existence of an actual King Arthur, the Welsh maintained a tradition of folklore that highlighted a leader named Arthur. Most early medieval chroniclers in England, such as Gildas, Nennius, and Bede, discussed the major battles between the Britons and Saxons in the sixth century, most often highlighting the battle at Badon Hill as an important victory for the Britons. The most contemporaneous chronicler of Arthur's lifetime was Gildas, who born in Wales, dated his own birth to the battle of Badon Hill in 516.[5] Gildas did not mention Arthur and attributes the defeat over the Saxons to another warlord, Ambrosius Aurelianus.[6] Twelfth-century chronicler Gerald of Wales argued that Gildas omitted Arthur from his chronicle because he disliked his character:

> The Britons maintain that, when Gildas criticized his own people so bitterly, he wrote as he did because he was so infuriated by the fact that King Arthur had killed his own brother, who was a Scottish chieftain. When he heard of his brother's death, or so the Britons say, he threw into the sea a number of outstanding books which he had written in their praise and about Arthur's achievements. As a result you will find no book which gives an authentic account of that great prince.[7]

In this description, Gerald of Wales explained the absence of Arthur in his contemporary's chronicle; he then reintroduced the king himself. Like Gildas, *The Anglo-Saxon Chronicle* made reference to an Ambrosius Aurelianus who led the Britons to victory against the Saxons at Badon Hill in the sixth century.[8] Bede, writing in the eighth century, provided a similar account of the battle and its participants:

> Their leader at this time was Ambrosius Aurelianus, a man of good character and the sole survivor of Roman race from the catastrophe ... Under his leadership the Britons took up arms, challenged their conquerors to battle, and with God's help inflicted defeat on them. Thenceforward victory swung first to one side and then to the other, until the battle of Badon Hill, when the Britons made a considerable

slaughter of the invaders.⁹

Ninth-century chronicler Nennius provided the first account of Arthur as a historical figure. In his *Historia Brittonum*, Nennius describes Arthur as a sixth-century Christian king and attributed to him the victory over the Saxons in the battle of Badon Hill.¹⁰ This was the first time that Arthur is credited with that victory. Nennius claimed that Arthur led the Britons against the Saxons in twelve battles. He thus advanced the idea of Arthur as a Christian king but did not discuss him as a figure beyond realistic historical proportions. Later medieval sources incorporated Arthur as a Christian leader into the chivalric ideal:

> Then it was, that the magnanimous Arthur, with all the kings and military force of Britain, fought against the Saxons. And though there were many more noble than himself, yet he was twelve times chosen their commander, and was as often conqueror.¹¹

By the twelfth century, Geoffrey of Monmouth and his contemporaries had adopted the view of Arthur as the great sixth-century warlord, and two theories about him emerged.

William of Malmesbury¹² discounted the growing reputation of Arthur as the quintessential leader of his era, whereas Geoffrey of Monmouth took up and developed the tradition of Arthur's legendary status. This became the dominant view for nearly four centuries. Geoffrey's *Historia Regum Britanniae*, written in 1136 for the Anglo-Norman court, was highly suggestive of the past and present glory of the English monarchy.¹³ *The Historia* was an account of the glorious efforts and triumphs of early English kings, with special emphasis on Arthur. In describing Arthur's death, Geoffrey of Monmouth claimed:

> Arthur himself, our renowned King, was mortally wounded and was carried off to the Isle of Avalon, so that his wounds might be attended to. He handed the crown of Britain over to his cousin Constantine, the son of Cador Duke of Cornwall: this in the year 542 after our Lord's Incarnation.¹⁴

Geoffrey incorporated the lore of Arthur's reign and the prophecy that he would return one day to rule all of England again. His history promoted the idea of Arthur as the epitome of a just ruler and the measure for future kings. Merriman states: "In the *Historia*, the vague cultural hero of Celtic tradition has become an actualized Christian king, a champion of women, and a righter of wrongs."¹⁵ The impact of this work was immediately felt in the subsequent reign of Henry II. He began the effort of English kings to assume the role of Arthur's successor. Henceforth, it was Geoffrey of Monmouth's account of Arthur as a historical and legendary hero that prevailed through the reigns of the early Tudors.

The most encyclopedic medieval source of Arthuriana is Sir Thomas Malory's

*Le Morte D'Arthur* (1485), which he wrote during his imprisonment.[16] His account was the culmination of Geoffrey of Monmouth and his successors' efforts to blend the history and legend of Arthur. In a synthesis of French and English accounts of the events of Arthur's life, Malory tried to compile the most comprehensive collection of stories about Arthur. He included Arthur's more legendary qualities while attempting to provide a historically credible depiction of him and his knights' lives.[17] Arriving late in the era of Arthurian enthusiasm, Malory's text was widely read and no doubt influenced the kings of his and subsequent generations. By the end of the fifteenth century, Arthur's legendary exploits were widely accepted as historically accurate; they were certainly offered as fact by the English kings hoping to benefit from their affiliation with the hero. From the time of Henry II onward, kings of England were increasingly intrigued by Arthur and his command over the people. They were specifically interested in the respect he received from his nobles, which they wished to emulate. Some monarchs, such as Henry VII (1485–1509), sought to solidify their questionable claims to the throne. Others, like Edward III (1327–1377), were so fascinated by the ideal of chivalry that they tried to incorporate its practices into their lives and those of the members of their courts.

The degree to which a king appealed to Arthur for authority varied, but Arthurian mythology remained a factor in English reigns throughout the later Middle Ages.[18] Henry II (1154–1189) tried to validate his authority by researching the lives of his Anglo and Norman predecessors. He unsuccessfully sought Arthur's remains, which Edward I (1272-1307) ceremoniously declared he found. These efforts to tie the post-conquest English monarchy to a pre-existing mythology of the people of England strengthened both the myth and the crown. Those who remained wary of the Norman court after William's conquest were more inclined to support a monarch who tied himself to their legendary king. Likening himself to the British representative amongst the Nine Worthies enabled the king to establish a relationship between himself and his subjects. This worked to diminish the animosity between the conqueror and those he conquered.[19] Furthermore, the myth itself experienced repeated renaissances through the continued interest of successive English kings.

Between 1154 and 1547,[20] English kings can be divided into greater and lesser Arthurian enthusiasts. His greatest champions were Edward I, Edward III, and Henry VII, whereas others, like Henry II and Henry VIII, manipulated Arthurian legend for political gain to a lesser degree. Some kings, such as Richard I and Richard III, demonstrated characteristics of the chivalrous ruler but did not seem to incorporate the mythology associated with Arthur into their reigns as much as others. Richard I participated in tournaments and Richard III demonstrated shrewdness as a ruler; however, neither seems to have made the connection between demonstrating chivalry and formally utilizing Arthurian mythology for political gain.

Edward I was the first great Arthurian enthusiast of the medieval English monarchs. He focused on Arthur's political and military persona and incorporated it into his own public image. Fourteenth-century English chronicler Nicholas Trivet described Edward as a very strong leader:

> He was a man of tried prudence in the transaction of affairs, devoted from his earliest years to the practice of arms. Hence he had won that fame as a knight in diverse lands that gave him a transcendent place among Christian princes. He was persuasive and ready in speech, in spite of his lisp. His long arms with their powerful and agile play enabled him to become a swordsman second to none.[21]

Edward I undertook considerable efforts to link himself to Arthur for a variety of politically motivated reasons. First, he wanted to extend his power throughout the island. Once Edward had conquered much of Wales, he associated himself with Arthur, the British hero, to make himself a more appealing leader to his new subjects.[22] He tried to lessen the strain between the English crown and the Welsh people by embracing their local mythology and expanding it to include the English, as well. He transferred the prophecy of Arthur's return and the significance of his successor to include rule over England, in addition to Wales. Further, by associating himself with Arthur, Edward established the notion of the English crown as both legitimate and chivalrous, legitimate in that the English king was the rightful heir to the crown and chivalrous in that he was the cultural and literary successor to Arthur.

> Now are the islanders all joined together,
> And Albany [Scotland] reunited to the royalties
> Of which King Edward is proclaimed lord.
> Cornwall and Wales are in his power,
> And Ireland the great at his will.
> There is neither king nor prince of all the countries
> Except King Edward, who has thus united them;
> Arthur had never the fiefs so fully.[23]

Here, Edward I is not only Arthur's heir, but has surpassed him as a leader. His triumph in Wales made Edward I and his successors the rightful rulers there, which was reinforced when he embraced Arthur's legacy. In an effort to liken himself to Arthur, he also built up his image as a chivalrous ruler. He did this with the introduction of tournaments and with grand festivals like those on the continent.[24] These eventually grew into Arthurian 'round table' tournaments where he and his nobles would perform as Arthur and his knights. These tournaments were meant to emulate the civilized manner of fighting that Arthur would have presumably participated in. The anachronistic nature of this effort reflects the shift in understanding of Arthur throughout the Middle Ages. Arthur, as a sub-Roman chieftain, would not have been involved in the courtly behavior described in late medieval literature. Christopher Dean argues: "Perhaps it was the wish on the part of some knights to have more carefully controlled encounters that prompted an appeal to the perceived ideas of Arthurian chivalry."[25] Edward even had his own round table made.[26] Edward I and his wife, Eleanor, would also dress as Arthur and Guinevere to establish themselves as the ideal chivalric couple.[27]

Edward I also tried to link himself to Arthur through the arts.[28] Like several of his successors, he commissioned Arthurian plays and works of art, such as tapestries, wall paintings, and decorative shields.[29] Both Henry III and Henry V claimed to have Arthur's sword, which celebrated their military glories, but Edward I claimed to have Arthur's crown, which signified his political prowess.[30] Edward I took the crown after conquering Wales and held a solemn ceremony where the crown was placed in Westminster Abbey. Dean describes this as an effort meant to represent Edward I as Arthur's successor:

> This action was intended to crush Welsh hopes of Arthur's return, as well as to symbolize Edward's sovereignty over Wales just as the removal of the coronation stone of Scone in 1296 was to symbolize his sovereignty over Scotland.[31]

In 1327, when Edward III took the English throne, he followed in his grandfather's footsteps by using Arthurian myth to develop his power.[32] Few kings were considered as chivalrous a leader in the medieval period as Edward III, whose reputation rivaled that of Richard I, the Lionheart.[33] Like Edward I, Edward III held 'round table' tournaments to promote the role of the chivalrous knights. His contemporary, Jean Froissart, described the great ceremony with which the king would enter into battle:

> The king then mounted a small palfrey, having a white wand in his hand, and attended by his two marshals on each side of him: he rode [at] a foot's pace through all the ranks, encouraging and intreating [sic] the army, that they would guard his honor and defend his right. He spoke sweetly, and with such a cheerful countenance, that all who had been dispirited were directly comforted by seeing and hearing him.[34]

This passage describes Edward III's constant effort to be accepted as a chivalrous leader. His appreciation of Arthur was seen both on and off the battlefield.

Edward III would dress as Arthur at festivals and encouraged his nobles to assume the role of the famous knights of Arthurian narratives.[35] He worked to establish a relationship between his nobles and the crown like Arthur had with his knights of the round table. In 1344, he decided to erect a building to house his round table.³⁶ Although the building was never completed nor the Order of the Round Table founded, he did create the Order of the Garter in 1348, to recognize his closest allies and nobles for their dedication to the king and his chivalric code. A mythology around the founding of the order also developed. Edward was supposed to have defended the honor of a lady in his court, who had lost her garter, by placing it around his arm. He disparaged those who might chastise her and encouraged his knights to follow his lead. Edward adopted the Arthurian tale of *Sir Gawain and the Green Knight* in which Gawain, Arthur's nephew and knight, wears a girdle, as symbol of his chivalric shortcomings. King Arthur himself refashions, authorizing it as a sign of his bravery and honor:

> The lord king and all the others stood up together, and having been offered the book, the lord king, after touching the Gospels, took a corporal oath that he himself, at a certain time appointed for this…would begin a Round Table, in the same manner and estate as the lord Arthur, formerly King of England, maintained it, namely to the number of 300 knights, a number always to be maintained.³⁷

Ultimately, the creation of this order is representative of the good relations Edward III prized between the crown and his nobles.

Like his grandfather and many other medieval kings, Edward III commissioned artwork featuring Arthur. Edward was similarly placed in the art of the time as an Arthurian figure.³⁸ He developed his ties to Arthur out of a sense of chivalric duty but, more importantly, he recognized how he could benefit from a connection to the legendary king. As the second Prince of Wales, Edward III had to work to maintain his control there. He was able to achieve this through his relationship with his nobles in Wales and throughout England. With the Order of the Garter and his military achievements in France and at home, Edward III successfully likened himself to Arthur and his nobles to Arthur's knights. Eventually the reputation of his similarity to their beloved Arthur disseminated to the people of his realm. During his reign, Arthurian literature reflected the political atmosphere of the times. The effects of the Hundred Years War were visible in Malory's text.³⁹ In his work, Arthur's military exploits resembled those of Edward III's in France. Michael Prestwich describes Malory's displeasure in the ongoing wars in France by associating Edward III with Arthur's overzealous military endeavors:

> In the later years of the reign an elaborate, alliterative *Morte Arthure* simultaneously glorified war and condemned Arthur's pride, ambition, and covetousness, plainly reflecting an increasingly ambiguous popular reaction to the French war.⁴⁰

Prestwich's description of Edward III highlights his negative qualities and likens them to Arthur's character flaws. Thus, Edward III's self-fashioning as Arthur affected his reign both positively and negatively.

Unlike Edward I or Edward III, who were direct heirs to the throne, Henry VII used his Arthurian connection to solidify his questionable claim to the crown.[41] Henry VII became king as the victor of the civil war between the Yorks and Lancasters. Polydore Vergil, an Italian visitor to his court and subsequent chronicler of the kings of England, described Henry VII having many of the kingly attributes typically ascribed to Arthur:

His spirit was distinguished, wise and prudent: his mind was brave and resolute and never, even at moments of the greatest danger, deserted him. He had a most pertinacious memory. Withal he was not devoid of scholarship. In government he was shrewd and prudent, so that no one dared to get the better of him through deceit or guile. He was gracious and kind and was as attentive to his visitors as he was of access. His hospitality was spendidly [sic] generous; he was fond of having foreigners at his court and he freely conferred favors on them.[42]

Although Vergil dismissed Arthur as mythological, his description of Henry VII echoed the language of Malory's portrayal of Arthur as a wise, just, and gracious ruler.

While Edward I and Edward III had to establish their power in Wales, Henry VII had less to prove to the people due to his Welsh ancestry. Being one quarter Welsh, his claim to the throne was "enhanced by the belief that in the Welsh blood of Henry of Richmond the very blood of Arthur had returned."[43] Like previous Welsh rulers, Henry VII played up his personal connection to Arthur, and thus he became the answer to the hero's prophetic return.[44] Henry VII suggested his connection to the mythological hero by adding him to a new Tudor coat of arms which illustrated his connection not only to Arthur but also to other great heroes, including Brutus and Aeneas. This made him the successor to Rome in addition to England. "The new Tudor monarch was claiming every heritage he could in order to legitimize his possession of the English throne."[45] Although Henry VII had to explore his Welsh ancestry in order to legitimize his claim to the throne, he could not delve too deeply into this issue. The Yorkist Edward IV had a more recent and stronger connection to Welsh royalty.[46]

Since he came to the throne at the end of a civil war, and many of his immediate predecessors had had to worry about usurpers, Henry VII was also concerned that his claims to power could be rejected, and he too would be overthrown.[47] By legitimizing himself through historical and legendary heroes, he strengthened his claim. He sought to establish a new Tudor dynasty and needed to make sure that his heir would succeed him. Like Edward IV before him, he hoped naming his eldest son Arthur would aid him in this effort.[48]

Although the Prince of Wales died before he could succeed his father, Henry VII's younger son, Henry VIII, did follow in his tradition of exploring their connection to Arthur. Henry VIII commissioned Arthurian artwork, too, and also dressed like Arthur at court balls.[49] Due to a lack of interest by later monarchs, Henry VIII was the last English king to be an Arthurian enthusiast.[50]

Monarchs of the early modern period sought stability through gaining colonies and nation-building. Thus, they were less interested in tying their genealogies back to Arthur for legitimacy. Although succession remained an issue for Renaissance monarchs, more modern concepts of identity that focused on the individual, rather than genealogy, prevailed at this time. Moreover, a female sovereign was less inclined to justify her power through the fabled return of an ancient king that she could not embody in her reign as queen. Thus, Elizabeth I was certainly unlikely to project an image of the medieval courtly lady, since her political objective was to be accepted as being as capable as a man in her position. The opinion of Arthur as the ideal ruler consequently had diminished by the end of the Tudor dynasty. Italian chronicler Polydore Vergil treated Arthur as strictly a legendary figure during Henry VII's reign.[51] By the middle of Elizabeth's reign, Raphaell Hollinshed returned to the early chroniclers' notion of Arthur as a historical king, but doubted the legendary feats and attributes credited to him:

> Of this Arthur manie things are written beyond credit, for that there is no ancient authoritie that confirmeth the same: but surelie as may be thought he was some woorthie man, and by all likelihood a great enimie to the Saxons, by reason whereof the Welshmen which are the verie Britains indeed, have him in famous remembrance.[52]

Some sixteenth-century chroniclers, like Hollinshed, relegated Arthur to ancient history. After Henry VIII's reign, however, Arthur generally came to be appreciated as a mythological figure and was no longer pursued as a means of justifying political power by the English crown.[53]

Nonetheless, the legend of Arthur and his Round Table was very important to English rulers of the later medieval period. From the aftermath of the Norman conquest to the accession of Edward I, Arthur developed from an acknowledged historical figure into an icon in the collective English and Welsh memory. As interest in Arthur grew, so did the legends associated with him, thereby expanding his reputation beyond realistic historical proportions. This was demonstrated by both the manner in which medieval historians dealt with Arthur and that in which English kings anachronistically looked back with nostalgia to a time of chivalry that never was. The earliest chroniclers mentioned him briefly as a minor king. However, the decision by Geoffrey of Monmouth to elevate Arthur's importance in the history of England created a new perspective of him. Subsequently, a shift in the manner in which English kings treated him occurred. Thomas Malory continued in this tradition by creating a comprehensive Arthurian chronicle.

Whereas some earlier monarchs depended upon the external force of association with legendary figures to establish their power, the relative stability of the Tudor and subsequent dynasties reduced the need for such outside help. This is why medieval English kings who understood how to manipulate the Arthurian legend obtained power through it which later rulers would find in the stability of their longer-lived hereditary dynasties. The view of Arthur as a historical or mythic figure correlates directly with the perception and adoption of him by English kings. Arthur, thus, transitioned from a minor warlord to a mythical-historical figure, and eventually to simply a legend. This transition reflects the early dependence and eventual abandonment of Arthur by late medieval monarchs, in which he shifted from a source of power to a national foundation myth.

*UNIVERSITY OF MISSOURI – KANSAS CITY*

NOTES

[1] Geoffrey of Monmouth, *The History of the Kings of Britain*, (London and New York: Penguin, 1966), 212.
[2] Christopher Dean, *Arthur of England: English Attitudes to King Arthur and the Knights of the Round Table in the Middle Ages and the Renaissance*, (Toronto: U of Toronto P, 1987), 7.
[3] A. D. Carr, *Medieval Wales*, (London: Macmillan, 1995), 4.
[4] James Douglas Merriman, *The Flower of Kings*, (Lawrence: UP of Kansas, 1973), 11.
[5] Joseph R. Strayer, *Dictionary of the Middle Ages, Vol. 1*, (New York, Charles Scribner's Sons, 1982), 564.
[6] Strayer, 564.
[7] Gerald of Wales, *The Description of Wales*, (London: Penguin, 1978), 259.
[8] Michael Swanton, *The Anglo-Saxon Chronicle*, (New York: Routledge, 1988).
[9] Bede, *Ecclesiastical History of the English People*, (New York: Penguin, 1990), 64.
[10] Nennius, *Historia Brittonum*, (London: Phillmore and Co., 1980), 51.
[11] Nennius, 50.
[12] Strayer, 565.
[13] Strayer, 565.
[14] Geoffrey of Monmouth, 261.
[15] Merriman, 12.
[16] Thomas Malory, *Le Morte D'Arthur*, (New York: The Modern Library, 1999).
[17] Elizabeth J. Bryan, Introduction to *Le Morte D'Arthur*, (New York: The Modern Library,

1999), vii.

[18] Dean, 44.

[19] Dean, 44.

[20] The period of 1154 to 1547 indicates the time between the beginning of Henry II's reign to the end of Henry VIII's.

[21] Nicholas Trivet in A. F. Scott's *Everyone A Witness: The Plantagenet Age, Commentaries of an Era*, (New York: Thomas Y. Crowell Co, 1975), 7.

[22] Juliet Vale, *Edward III and Chivalry* (Exeter: Short Run P, 1982), 18.

[23] Peter of Langtoft, in *The Oxford Illustrated History of the British Monarchy*, eds. John Cannon and Ralph Griffiths (Oxford: Oxford UP, 1998), 276.

[24] Vale, 16.

[25] Dean, 39.

[26] Vale, 19.

[27] Vale, 17.

[28] Dean, 47-48.

[29] Vale, 15.

[30] Vale, 17.

[31] Dean, 55.

[32] Michael Prestwich, *The Three Edwards: War and State in England, 1272 – 1377*, (London and New York: Routledge, 1980), 204-5.

[33] A. F. Scott, *Everyone A Witness: The Plantagenet Age, Commentaries of an Era*, (New York: Thomas Y. Crowell Co., 1975), 4-5.

[34] John Froissart in *Everyone A Witness: The Plantagenent Age*, 10.

[35] Vale, 55.

[36] Vale, 77.

[37] Adam Murimth in *The Oxford Illustrated History of the British Monarchy*, John Cannon and Ralph Griffiths (Oxford: Oxford UP, 1998), 285.

[38] Dean, 47-48.

[39] Paul E. Szarmach, M. Teresa Tavormira, and Joel T. Rosenthal, *Medieval England, An Encyclopedia*, (New York and London: Garland, 1998), 470.

[40] Prestwich, 211.

[41] Ralph A. Griffiths and Roger S. Thomas, *The Making of the Tudor Dynasty*, (Gloucester: Alan Sutton, 1985), 189.

[42] Polydore Vergil in *Everyone A Witness: The Plantagenet Age*, 21-23.

[43] Millican in Merriman, *The Flower of Kings*. 35.

[44] Dean, 27.

[45] Dean, 46.

[46] Dean, 28.

[47] Paul Thomas, *Authority and Disorder in Tudor Times, 1483 – 1603*, (Cambridge: Cambridge UP, 1999), 1.

[48] Griffiths and Thomas, 190.

[49] Dean, 47-48.

[50] Dean, 28.

[51] Strayer, 565

[52] Raphaell Hollinshed, *The History of England* (New York: AMS P, 1965), 574.

[53] Thomas, 3.

# Anglo-Saxonism and Charles Kingsley's *Hereward the Wake: Last of the English*

Robert Sirabian

> Those who professed themselves unable to believe in the reality of human progress ought to cheer themselves up, as the students under examination had conceivably been cheered up, by a short study of the Middle Ages. The hydrogen bomb, the South African Government, Chiang Kaishek, Senator McCarthy himself, would then seem a light price to pay for no longer being in the Middle Ages. Had people ever been as nasty, as self-indulgent, as dull, as miserable, as cocksure, as bad at art, as dismally ludicrous, or as wrong...?
>
> Kingsley Amis, *Lucky Jim*[1]

As Claire Simmons argues in *Reversing the Conquest*,[2] by the beginning of the twentieth century, England's Anglo-Saxon past had become less of a myth fostered by literature and more of a factual reality validating England's position as a world power. Jim Dixon's observation in *Lucky Jim* reflects a twentieth-century reaction to the Anglo-Saxons, in part fueled by an anti-imperialist temperament.[3] "The reality of human progress" at the end of the nineteenth century was, in many circles, not measured against an illusory Anglo-Saxon Golden Age, or the medieval notion of Merrie Old England, but confirmed by a past presented as fact that cemented ideas affirming national character and bloodline.

The Victorians, however, still debated the significance of the Anglo-Saxon period and the Norman Conquest as they tried to connect England's past to its contemporary national identity while also validating its future. Norman Vance[4] points out that in the 1860s Anglo-Saxonism was in historical and antiquarian vogue, signaled by William Theed's statue of Victoria and Albert in Anglo-Saxon dress. In the same era, E. A. Freeman published his *History of the Norman Conquest*, a history, Vance notes that is a patriotic nod to the fall of Teutonic England (100). As England's imperial mission intensified during the last quarter of the century, the past was significant for justifying colonial expansion as a historical continuum that saw the past values of the national origin and character fulfilled. If England was once conquered, it was now the conqueror. At the same time, though, Queen Victoria's reign and the King Alfred millennium celebration still fostered a longing for a return to an Anglo-Saxon Golden Age lost in defeat.

Following Edward Bulwer-Lytton's *Harold* (1848), a nostalgic homage to England's last Saxon King, *Hereward the Wake: Last of the English* (1866)[5] centers on the last of the Anglo-Saxons, a guerilla fighter who resists the Norman Conquest despite its inevitability. Patriotic readings of the novel view Hereward and his men as holding out valiantly as free English until the end, or as Hereward says, "[Playing] out the lost game to the last" (400). Most contemporary readers see the novel as promoting a national myth of origin. In addition, they see the novel as confusing in its attempt to depict Hereward as a national hero since his ultimate demise results, not from military defeat, but from his own moral failure to remain faithful to his wife Torfrida and from his acknowledgement of William as England's true leader of England.[6] Perhaps more problematic is how Hereward's fall fits with the novel's larger argument that the Conquest was the acting out of a divine plan combining God's will and evolutionary progression. As Andrew Sanders argues the case, "David sins with Bathsheba; Hereward with Torfrida. Red-blooded heterosexuals both may prove themselves to be, but they are also unworthy of the moral responsibility thrust upon them by the national mission entrusted to them."[7] This reading explains Hereward's personal failure as part of a larger divine pattern, but the novel raises doubts about its own view of the relationship between past and present.

The tensions or oppositions in *Hereward the Wake* do not signal its lack of unity or confused argument. They represent the inability of a literary narrative to order and resolve competing ideas neatly about Anglo-Saxonism, as either a justification of progress or as a check against the problems associated with progress by invoking the past.[8] Although *Hereward the Wake* asserts a progressive view of history, it simultaneously attaches to this view the notion of an Anglo-Saxon Golden Age as a check against nineteenth-century social ills resulting from rapid social change. More specifically, it fuses these competing views, showing them both to be valid ways of understanding the Norman Conquest that reflected the fermenting and changing political and cultural attitudes and ideas embodied in nineteenth-century Anglo-Saxonism. In this way, the novel reveals the shifting and competing ideas about the relationship between past and present. Although holding two competing views of Anglo-Saxonism appears contradictory, the novel combines these views into the same historical continuum yet leaves each view as a viable vision defining national identity. While Scott's *Ivanhoe* suggests that Saxon and Norman can integrate peacefully to improve upon the character of each, this integration is more self-consciously suspect in *Hereward the Wake*. Presenting history as both linear and cyclical, the narrative resists asserting one view as absolute or sacrificing the distinctions of English and Norman within a hybrid solution. The Victorian historical novel demonstrates that only by understanding how literature reflects social and cultural change and offers imaginative solutions to problems of national identity can we come closest to an understanding of how the past was used nostalgically as a reaction against progress and alternatively to justify it.

*Hereward the Wake* begins by claiming a progressive view of history. Victorians such as Macaulay interpreted history as progress, and in their evolutionary view of history, the Anglo-Saxons had reached their zenith by the time of the Conquest. Although they had fought bravely and valiantly, the stronger, more socially and politically adept Normans asserted their right to rule. Although Anglo-Saxon society had run its course, the notable racial, social, and cultural characteristics of the Anglo-Saxon people were carried through successive generations to the present. This progressive view promoted and justified England's imperial mission and status in the world.

Hereward's position as romantic outlaw and nationalist leader, however, presents a competing view of Anglo-Saxon England as a Golden Age. Introduced by the novels of Sir Walter Scott (although Scott's fiction is more complex than this one reading), the nostalgia for the past was a call for a return to England's past where Englishmen were free and created political and social institutions that ensured and protected that freedom.[9] The repressive yoke of the Normans after the Conquest destroyed Anglo-Saxon society and repressed its freedoms. Voices such as Matthew Arnold's speaker in *Stanzas from the Grand Chartreuse* (1852),[10] Thomas Carlyle in *Characteristics* (1831), and Tennyson's King Arthur in the *Idylls* (1833-69) lament the loss of the old order and the uncertainty of a new one. In *Past and Present* (1843), Carlyle advocates a return to an industrial feudalism by having Captains of Industry assume the role of medieval lords. For numerous writers, Anglo-Saxonism functioned as a check or correction to progress and registers a concern over the social, economic, and political problems unanswered from 1840s through the 1860s.

*Hereward the Wake* promotes contending views of Anglo-Saxonism within its main argument about the historical movement from primitive romanticism to civilization. Placed in opposition are the lowlands and highlands. The highlands, associated with Sir Walter Scott's fiction, produced individuals or fictional heroes with greater sensibilities and respect for the power of Nature and the Creator behind it, which fostered self-restraint and intellect. The magical and fantastic are products of their poetic and imaginative qualities. By contrast, the inhabitants of the lowlands, the narrator states, had no reverence for Nature, taking the position of lording over it. Without the thoughtfulness and reverence for Nature and the force behind it, the "unseen" died out within them. Only civilization and religion can prevent the eventual sink into brutality, and this brutality or roughness eventually leads to the conquering of the lowlanders. Having stated this, the narrator also makes it clear that the lowlanders had admirable characteristics, particularly their ruggedness, bravery, and cunning, which allowed them to resist to the vices of civilization that allow the silly and weak to survive in the contemporary age. As *Hereward's* narrator notes, the demise of the Anglo-Saxons results from their being "priest-driven, and enslaved by their own aristocracy" (6), victims, as it were, of their own civilizing.

Kingsley's evolutionary explanation, however, is tempered with divine origin, expressed in a telling passage from the preface. After acknowledging that change as a result of the Conquest came at a brutal price, the narrator asks the following question: "Is it not to say that men's crimes are not merely overruled by, but necessary to, the gracious designs of Providence; and that—to speak plainly—the Deity has made this world so ill that He is forced at times to do ill that good may come?" (11). The movement of history in the novel from romance to civilization comes at a terrible price, and the narrator's question raises an uncertainty about the ends justifying the means, and about the end itself—whether or not the Conquest was a necessary step to England's present-day position as an imperial power. If Hereward's moral failure and defeat were divinely preordained at the hands of a random or even cruel Deity, then England's defeat is difficult to explain and justify within a larger historical pattern that supports its present and future nationalistic purpose. Furthermore, this deterministic pattern minimizes the significance of individual free will, a hallmark of inherent human freedom and Englishness itself.

The text's claim for a progressive view of history is grounded in the narrator's claim that the "Anglo-Saxon race was wearing out" (6). This point is underscored by Hereward's concerns about Englishmen's lack of knowledge about warfare and his complaints about England's lack of effective leadership after the reign of Canute. As *Hereward the Wake* opens, several years before 1066, Anglo-Saxon society is depicted as in decline and ripe for invasion. Hereward leaves England because he sees its institutions as ineffective and corrupt, particularly the church, and he resorts to rebellious behavior as an expression of his disdain for incapable authority and his English identity.

When Hereward returns to England after living as a mercenary outlaw in Flanders, he tries to raise an army to fight the "master-general of his age, William of Normandy" (305). The English, however, are ignorant about military tactics: "Their armies were little more than tumultuous levies, in which men marched and fought under local leaders, often divided by local jealousies. The commissariats of the armies seem to have been so worthless, that they had to plunder friends as well as foes as they went along....And even the local leaders were not over-well obeyed" (305). Unable to field a professional army because of a lack of organization and communication, particularly after the defeat at Hastings and Harold's death, Hereward must lead a guerilla war. Only through the pressure of outside invaders and Hereward's leadership does the outlaw band manage to frustrate William's armies as long as they do. When the Danish forces whom Hereward attempts to sway to his cause decide that the outlaw's fight is not theirs and sail home, he knows that his resistance is only a delaying tactic of inevitable defeat. When living in the Greenwood as an outlaw with Hereward and his men, Torfrida observes that this idea of valor is far from admirable: "She was discovering the fact, which her nation have more than once discovered since, that the stupid valour [sic] of the Englishman never knows when it is beaten; and, sometimes, by self-satisfied ignorance, succeeds in not being beaten after all" (448). This point is made earlier in the preface as well, when the narrator notes that Hereward and his men, "not knowing, like true Englishmen, when they were beaten" (4), fought to their last man.

The lack of effective leadership is perhaps the most commonly used reason for the Norman Conquest and cause for the invocation of the character of Alfred in the nineteenth-century. The affirmation of Victoria's reign and England's world position became a means of reversing the Conquest's meaning, demonstrating that a historical setback had been overcome. The leadership problem of pre-Conquest England was not due to a need for more leaders, as Hereward points out during the great meeting with the Danes at the outlaw camp at Ely. When Danish king Sweyn Ulfsson shouts that England needed three men like Hereward, he laughs and replies, "Thou are wrong for once, wise king. We have failed, just because there were a dozen men as good as I, every man wanting his own way; and too many cooks have spoiled the broth. What we wanted is...one like thee, to take us all by the back of the neck and shake us soundly, and say, 'Do that, or die!'" (365).

Early in the novel, when Hereward is serving King Ranald of Waterford and meets up with his nephews, he tells them that Harold, although a limited leader, is England's only hope, with the Danish line of kings dead. It is through a natural dying out of royal bloodlines that Hereward becomes England's last leader, a role he initially rejects. Significant is Hereward's status by blood as the last of the English; the novel explains the Conquest in terms of race by deemphasizing a Golden Age of pure Anglo-Saxon bloodline in favor of Anglo-Dane-Norman heritage. It is the Danes to whom Hereward must appeal for help, and by the time of the Conquest, the Norman social influence was pronounced. Englishness was, in fact, a mixture of Saxon, Dane, and Norman, and in the nineteenth century, "the real distraction in dealing with Saxon England lay in the fact that it was exclusively [presented as] Saxon" (Sanders, "'Utter Indifference'?" 173).

The numerous descriptions of nature, some of Kingsley's best writing, reinforce an evolutionary view of history. As Hereward is rowing to Crowland, where he will dedicate himself to England's struggle as a monk-knight, nature is shown to be somber and teeming with life, but ultimately a struggle of the fittest predicated unsentimentally on violence: "Out of the reeds, like an arrow, shot the peregrine, singled one luckless mallard form the flock, caught him up, struck him stone dead with one blow of his terrible heel, and swept his prey with him into the reeds again" (269). But nature is also revealed to be God's creation. When relics are being used to try to appease the Dane invaders of Peterborough, "a thousand skylarks rose from off the fen and chanted their own chant aloft, as if appealing to heaven against that which man's greed, and man's rage, and man's superstition, had made of this fair earth of God" (341). The paganism and superstition of the Anglo-Saxons and Anglo-Danes is a sign of their primitivism, yet the narrator is equally suspicious of the Catholicism introduced by the Normans, who are seen as controlled by the Pope. The Anglo-Saxon fear of nature is well-founded, but the idea of lording over nature, explained in the preface, is shown to be foolhardy. Nature has its own hierarchy and order, and it reveals the same evolutionary forces that will cause human societies to be replaced.

Hereward's ultimately futile guerilla war against William, his capitulation and betrayal of his wife through his marriage to Alftruda, and his death fulfill the progressive historical pattern the novel proposes. Even its ending seemingly looks forward to a new Norman order, more advanced and stronger than the Anglo-Saxon society it replaced. Michael Young,[11] however, persuasively argues that *Hereward the Wake's* proposed historical explanation of progress as the movement from romance to civilization is actually reversed, that romance (and rebellion) is actually sanctioned by civilization and as a result diminishes the novel's argument for history as natural progress: "Social rebellion on a historical scale, with its specific grievances and a particular cause, is naturalized and generalized, reduced to the dimension of a transient phase stripped of all serious threat" (181-82).

But rather than offer a deceptive or inept attempt at myth-making, the novel self-consciously incorporates a counterview of the Conquest by emphasizing an Anglo-Saxon Golden Age whose virtues are freedom, social cohesiveness, heroism, paternalism, chivalry, and masculinity. By looking back, the novel questions the virtues of progress, critiquing the forces of industrialization that define progress in economic terms as well as the imperial mission itself. In his study of chivalry and its influence on the Victorians,[12] Mark Girouard draws connections between the gentleman code and imperialism, noting that key proponents of the Empire desired to create societies that were "paternalistic, hierarchic, and rural" (225), free of perceived excessive democratic controls. Yet Girouard also notes that many imperialists were not readily associated with the "ideals of chivalry" because, for one reason, they often were in positions of power. The complexity of the colonial enterprise made it resistant to the easy application of ideals or simple concepts: "Indeed, chivalrous metaphors could be more naturally used for those who tilted against the Empire rather than for it" (227-28). While Hereward's rebellion may not be a "serious threat" in the context of the novel's plot, it does create, thorough a general set of values associated with a simpler time, an alternative view of the Conquest, which elicited more complex and varied reactions than a single view could contain.

The same narrator that proclaimed that the Anglo-Saxon race was "worn out" also claims that the men of Wessex were "the once conquering, and even to the last the most civilised [sic], race of Britain." After Hastings, he further explains, their Danish countrymen held out against the Normans until there were "none left to fight" (4). These men "never really bent their necks to the Norman yoke" under whose rule "those free institutions" were "in abeyance" (4). Here, the narrator recalls England's past as a time of pride and a period in which English identity and national identity were formed. A race that dies out is, at the same time, described as subjugated by an oppressive Norman yoke that denied English liberties. The Anglo-Saxons had built an ordered and free society, which was improved at various stages by the Danes. Although incompetent leaders and internal machinations caused disruptions and the times were often violent, kings such as Alfred and Canute exemplify the Anglo-Saxon achievements of law and order, stability and national cohesiveness. Beginning in the preface, then, the novel sets an alternative view of the Conquest alongside its assumed main view of history as progress.

Although the Anglo-Saxons are presented as a waning society, their character traits are shown to be admirable in contrast to the civilized Normans. The most significant of these is their expression of personal freedom, instinctual and divinely inspired. The novel presents a romantic, heroic view of this freedom by aligning the Anglo-Saxons with the land and by emphasizing their status as outlaws. What Torfrida views as "self-satisfied ignorance" is depicted throughout the novel as a quintessential English characteristic, the defense of God-given freedom, resistance to unjust authority, and courage in the face of overwhelming odds. Hereward's maturation in the novel from rebellious youth to outlaw hero is signaled by his eventual acceptance of the chivalric code and acceptance of national responsibility.

A key to Hereward's acceptance of the chivalric code is the practice of self-restraint. His early adventures slaying the giant bear, killing the giant of Cornwall, and achieving numerous military victories emphasize a romantic, heroic code predicated on masculine valor and bravery, but without self-restraint and discipline to check and guide the impulses of personal expressions of freedom, the implication is that the English (in 1066 or 1866) cannot survive as an organized society. Life in Flanders with Torfrida teaches Hereward the importance of restraint, not only in the application of physical force but also in temperament. Chivalry is associated with French (Norman) influence, yet Hereward adopts it more generally as his own and as representative of Anglo-Saxon values. Absolute freedom without some control is an unsustainable condition. The knighting of Hereward at the church of Crowland and the changing of the emblem of his shield from the white bear to a "W" formed from the knots of a monk's girdle demonstrate his conversion. The significance of Hereward's moniker, the Wake, underscores competing views of the Conquest. As a verb, "wake" means "a state or period of wakefulness," as well as the notion of keeping vigil or watching,[13] certainly describing the national responsibility Hereward assumes and a meaning that looks forward, not only to Hereward's resistance, but also to England's national mission. In its noun form, though, "wake" signifies a track left behind, which extends back in time.[14] Hereward's mission looks both forward and backward, combining present, future, and past.

Hereward's life in Flanders after his romantic adventures demonstrates the virtues of an ordered, paternalistic society in his service under the Marquis Baldwin. He does, however, conquer and subdue those who threaten the Marquis, a model of imperial power, yet he learns to apply the rules of chivalry in combat. One key episode that further throws doubt on a progressive view of history is when Hereward assists the Marquis Baldwin in defeating the "Free Frisians." The narrator makes it a point to tell readers that Hereward is unable to comprehend the significance of his actions. Instead of drawing a parallel between the Frisians and the English, two societies that value freedom and liberty, he views them as "simply savages, probably heathens, who would not obey their lawful lord, a gentleman and Christian; besides, renown, and possibly a little plunder, might be got by beating them into obedience" (152). The narrator, in revealing Hereward's thoughts, implies both regret for this loss of inherent freedom and an evolutionary justification for their defeat. But as admirable as their natural character might be, it is overshadowed by the interests of social evolution, supported by God's divine purpose. Ironically, this episode foreshadows what will happen to England, and the justification becomes equally suspect. Moreover, the example of the Free Frisians as savages who need civilizing casts doubt on England's current imperial mission as morally justified and beneficial to those who are enlightened.

Hereward's "civilizing" is attributed to the Norman (French) influence of Torfrida and his time in Flanders, but it is in the Greenwood that the novel presents an alternative to Norman civilization—a life close to nature driven by self-reliance and self-government: "Gradually, too, law and order arose among them, lawless as they were; that instinct of discipline and self-government, side by side, with that of personal independence, which is the peculiar mark, and peculiar strength, of the English character" (445). In the prelude, the narrator notes the corrupting influences of civilization, and the sections of the novel in the Greenwood take readers back to a Saxon past free from the political machinations and turmoil of the nineteenth century. It is also the characteristics represented by the outlaw—good humor, fair play, and equal justice—that are said to define life for the Victorians and form the basis of English education (446).

The novel's argument for the advancement of civilization is countered with a view of the past that is more harmonious, free, and just. Although law and order belong to the realm of civilization, here the difference is that they are instinctual and rooted in tradition, tempered by freedom and applied by self-government. Free from civilization's bureaucracies as well as institutional political jealousies and self-interest, the communal, rural Greenwood does offer an alternative, albeit mythic, to the Norman order and the waning Anglo-Saxon society. "Rural England in the late nineteenth century was of course already changing, an integral part of modern society. Yet it was rarely seen for what it was" (51), states Martin Weiner in *England Culture and the Decline of the Industrial Spirit 1850-1980*.[15] There was a nostalgic desire to see rural England as a timeless refuge from industrial upheaval (Weiner 51-2), a view clearly articulated in the outlaws' Greenwood sanctuary.

The actions of the Norman conquerors and William in particular again challenge the idea of William as England's leader. The brutal administration of Norman authority post-Conquest supports the "Norman yoke" theory. Although William demonstrates an understanding of the need for assimilation and fair treatment of his new subjects, he insists on establishing his absolute authority and overlooks the attitudes and actions of his own subordinates, who desire land and power. The rebellions that occurred after 1066, the narrator explains, are put down brutally by William, who left the English largely in the hands of his subordinates rather than fulfilling his promise of justice and fairness in ruling his newly conquered subjects. The Norman's brutality is underscored in the second-to-last chapter of the novel, which lists specific methods of torture used against the English after Hereward's death.

The alternate views of William are articulated when, on the one hand, Hereward himself admits to Torfrida that he is no match for William, "'the wisest man on earth'" (334), and alternatively when William is depicted as ruthless, barbaric, and egotistical. Furthermore, the narrative juxtaposes the outlaw society with the corrupt Norman order, invaders who use a strict social organization based on political self-interest to conquer, repress, and torture their subjects. When Hereward returns to England to take up the English cause, he views the English landscape of farms, enclosed fields, and rough fen, exclaiming, "A pleasant and peaceable country we have come back to" (250). This, along with additional descriptions, reminds readers of a country and people who, even amidst the invading Normans, had established an ordered society and achieved stability through fair institutions as well as self-government. Hereward's defeat at the hands of a capable, strong leader is supposed to mollify the sting of defeat and explain the progression of English society as a mixture of various bloodlines, but as the novel clearly shows, the Anglo-Saxons lose their society because of the Normans, described as having a "skin-deep yesterday's society" and being "invaders and tyrants" (542).

Hereward's moral lapse is at the crux of the novel's view of the Conquest's historical significance. The novel uses the muscular Christian hero Hereward and his outlaw band to make the overt patriotic statement of fighting for one's country even when defeat is at hand. Ultimately, it is the act of resistance that merits praise, rather than the outcome. Hereward himself acknowledges he is fighting for a lost cause, yet he becomes determined to play out the game until the end. But this heroic attitude also provides ready reasons to justify Hereward's defeat and moral lapse beyond the inevitability of circumstances.

Life in the Greenwood proves to be hard for Torfrida and Hereward, where, away from the forces of civilization, it becomes easy to lapse into a primitive way of living. Hereward's growth in novel from self-centered ruffian to chivalric monk-knight and defender of England is challenged by the outlaw life. As the narrator notes, "Away from law, from self-restraint, from refinement, from elegance, from the very sound of the church-going bell, they were sinking gradually down to the level of the coarse men and women whom they saw" (473). Forced to live as outlaws as a result of Norman tyranny, Hereward's social and moral lapse becomes justifiable, because personal independence and self-government are difficult to sustain without a larger social organization and institutions of law and religion. Again, the romance and civilization spheres seem to conflate. Certainly, the French influence on manners and elegance is evoked here, but civilization is surely identified with the England represented by Alfred and Canute, not that associated with William and the Normans. When discussing Abbot Thorold's ransom, Hereward replies, "What higher compliment can I pay to your vast worth, than making your ransom high accordingly, after the spirit of our ancient English laws?" (469). The Anglo-Saxons may not have been refined, but they were guided by law and religion, by self-government and traditions.

Most difficult to justify, however, is Hereward's unfaithfulness to his wife and capitulation to William, which explain Hereward's failure as personal weakness and historical inevitability. The narrator supplies a reason with an almost offhand comment that "He [Hereward] had been faithful to Torfrida—a virtue most rare in those days" (451). But having fallen out of love with Torfrida, even the heroic Hereward succumbs to Alftruda's charms and makes reconciliations with William, ending the resistance and abandoning his men. Rescuing the meaning of the Conquest through the "Norman yoke" theory is possible, but explaining moral failure within this theory is more difficult. The novel tries to do this by showing Hereward as a beaten man, stripped of love and spirituality, removed too long from "civilizing influences," all the effects of carrying a national burden.

But national heroes are expected to have superhuman resilience and strength. If the Anglo-Saxon Golden Age was one where heroic, masculine action was possible, then Hereward's personal failing places this possibility in question. Contributing to the tension between the pair is Torfrida's inability to give Hereward a son. Without an heir apparent, Hereward's legacy ends with his death, and the larger significance of his fight is diminished, making his resistance more of a personal battle than a national one. The main argument of the novel would place his failing with the larger divine scheme of punishment and historical redemption, but Hereward's unfaithfulness seems to define failure as his own choice: "Once in his life—for his other sins and were but sins of the age—the Father of men seems (if chroniclers say truth) to have put before this splendid barbarian good and evil, saying Choose! And he knew that evil was evil, and chose it nevertheless" (543). Could the narrator equivocate more than this? He distinguishes between types of sins, making Hereward's sin extraordinary; he separates himself, ironically, from the chroniclers, who may be wrong; and he describes Hereward as a "splendid barbarian," who might be expected to choose evil.

If the end of the English results from Hereward's own failure, then individuals are largely powerless to determine the course of their history, a view that would have added to Victorian doubt about the possibility of heroism and individual's ability to effect social change. The past, however, evoked a time when heroism was still possible. A "worn-out old man" with no spirit left and racked with guilt, Hereward is finally ambushed while asleep as a result of a plot by William's men, including Ivo Taillebois, who represents the cruel, vainglorious Norman leader; Hereward suffers an ignominious death, considering his life of adventure, service, and renown. The opening of the novel's final chapter answers the question laid out in the preface concerning

God's plan, yet this general statement avoids the dilemma of the means of God's plan by emphasizing the outcome: "And then the true laws of God's universe, peace and order, usefulness and life, will reassert themselves, as they have been waiting all along to do, hid in God's presence from the strife of men" (565). Evil and death seem to be a necessary condition of God's purpose; hence Hereward's fall as part of a divine plan. But while the fens are transformed by human hands (Sanders, *The Victorian Historical Novel* 166), Hereward is unable to save England, powerless and subjected to the violence and suffering engendered by a secret plan never revealed to him. The very notions of muscular Christianity, that the body should be trained and subjugated to God's will and that it can also be used for chivalrous action, conflict here. The complexity of relating the past to the present is signaled by the narrative's continual juxtapositions of historical theories, from its preface to its conclusion.

In the preface to the sixth edition of historian Sharon Turner's *The History of the Anglo-Saxons* (1836)[16], Turner uses a grafting metaphor to combine linear and cyclical notions of history:

> The Anglo-Saxons were deficient in the surprising improvements which their present descendents have attained; but unless they had acquired and exercised the valuable qualities, both moral and intellectual, which they progressively advanced to before their dynasty ceased, England would not have become that distinguished nation which, after the Norman graft on its original Saxon stock, it has since gradually led to be (quoted in Simmons 59).

This grafting model aptly explains the inclusion of both views of the Conquest presented in *Hereward the Wake*, since "a graft hybrid is an organism made up of two genetically distinct tissues due to fusion of host and donor (scion and stock) after grafting."[17] ("Graft" 281). By grafting the Golden Age or cyclical theory of history onto a progressive theory of history, the novel incorporates both views into a larger historical pattern while maintaining the values and meanings of each. Moreover, both in biology and human physiology, the purpose of grafting is to promote healing, repair, or improvement upon the original or host. Given the social and political flux in the nineteenth century, *Hereward the Wake* suggests a desire to include the various traits and characteristics of Englishness, rather than exclude some over others for the sake of political expediency or cultural vindication.

The novel's desire for inclusive readings of the Conquest is signaled most clearly in its conclusion, when Torfrida, Hereward's granddaughter, suggests a rewriting of Hereward's tomb and proposes a complimentary inscription for Norman Richard de Rulos, the first of the new Norman agriculture squires. Since Hereward's tombstone is burned in the fire at Crowland, Rulos suggests obtaining a new stone from Normandy and rewriting the original inscription: "Here lies the last of the English." But Torfrida suggests his stone read, "Here lies the last of the old English" (570).[18] Ironically, the Norman Rulos offers the inscription that invokes an Anglo-Saxon Golden Age of the heroic, romantic Hereward and of a society that instituted law and government. The draining and partitioning of the Fen for agriculture suggests a loss of natural, untamed nature that characterizes the early Anglo-Saxons and Danes. And this pattern of change will be repeated with more drastic, unsettling consequences following the shift from an agrarian to an industrial society. It is Torfrida, Hereward's descendent, who delimits that past as "old" and offers another inscription for Rulos's tombstone, which represents an emphasis on peace, cultural integration, and the virtues of progress sanctioned by God: "Here lies the first of the new English; who, by the inspiration of God, began to drain the Fens" (570). Although Torfrida's comments are given often emphasis, Rulos, the symbol of progress, honors the last of the English with his tombstone inscription—a nod to the importance of looking back to the order he has replaced. Hereward and Rulos's written and rewritten tombstones may be viewed as the facing leaves of a text, reconstructing the meaning between past and present and showing the inability of one narrative alone to explain the connections between past and present. In this way, Anglo-Saxonism is an idea, rather than a place. For the Victorians, who lived in an age when views were continually created and questioned, Anglo-Saxonism was an idea they confronted and assessed into the following century and which caused them to both justify their national mission and question it.

*UNIVERSITY OF WISCONSIN—STEVENS POINT*

NOTES

[1] Amis Kingsley, *Lucky Jim*, (Harmondsworth: Penguin, 1954), 87.
[2] Claire A. Simmons, *Reversing the Conquest: History and Myth in Nineteenth-Century British Literature*, (New Brunswick: Rutgers UP, 1990).
[3] Donald Scragg, "Introduction: The Anglo-Saxons: Fact and Fiction," to *Literary Appropriations of the Anglo-Saxons from the Thirteenth to the Twentieth Century*, eds. Donald Scragg and Carole Weinburg, (Cambridge: Cambridge UP, 2000), 1-21 (5-6).
[4] Norman Vance, *The Sinews of the Spirit: Ideals of Christian Manliness in Victorian Literature and Religious Thought*, (Cambridge: Cambridge UP, 1985).
[5] Charles Kingsley, *Hereward the Wake: Last of the English*, (London: Collins' Clear-Type P, n.d.). All citations to the text are from this edition.
[6] In *The Victorian Historical Novel 1840-1880* (New York" St. Martin's, 1979), Andrew

Sanders notes that "despite the care which marks the background research and the use of landscape and wild nature in *Hereward the Wake*, the novel as a whole is an amalgam of confused elements lacking a central logic and direction" (160). Michael Young, in "History as Myth: Charles Kingsley's *Hereward the Wake*" (*Studies in the Novel* 17 (1985): 174-88), argues that the novel assimilates "opposed elements into a structure that appears to be a coherent whole but which is actually only an illusion of unity, and leaves fundamental contradictions unresolved" (175). And in *The Sinews of the Spirit*, Norman Vance, while approving of Kingsley's overall handling of the historical Hereward, concedes that "Darwin and the historical record provided a convenient excuse for indulging in romantic primitivism" (99).

[7] Andrew Sanders, "'Utter Indifference'?: The Anglo-Saxons in the Nineteenth-Century Novel," in *Literary Appropriations of the Anglo-Saxons from the Thirteenth to the Twentieth Century*, eds. Donald Scragg and Carole Weinburg, (Cambridge: Cambridge UP, 2000), 157-73, (172).

[8] See Professor Dino Felluga's course syllabus (http://web.ics.purdue.edu/~felluga/medievalism/hypo3F99.html) on 19th Century Medievalism. His class discussions raise the question, "Can medievalism both affirm progress and simultaneously serve as a check against it?" I have used this fruitful approach to focus on Anglo-Saxonism and it particular concerns for *Hereward the Wake*.

[9] For example, consider King Alfred's unification of the English, development of a court system, and interest in education. Canute is also extolled as a strong leader who improved Anglo-Saxon society. See the preface of *Hereward*. Also, many nineteenth-century writers, such as Wordsworth (*Ecclesiastical Sonnets*), Dickens (*A Child's History of England*), and Bulwer-Lytton (*Harold: The Last of the Saxon Kings*), focus on Anglo-Saxon subjects and invoke Alfred and Canute as exemplary leaders.

[10] Arnold criticizes middle class values defined largely in terms of material progress, but in *The Function of Criticism at the Present Time*, he also sarcastically links these values to England's Anglo-Saxon heritage by questioning Sir Charles Adderley's claim, "Our old Anglo-Saxon breed, the best in the whole world." Quoted in William E. Butler, *Prose of the Victorian Period*, (Boston: Houghton Mifflin, 1958), 432.

[11] Michael Young, "History as Myth: Charles Kingsley's *Hereward the Wake*," in *Studies in the Novel* 17 (1985): 174-88.

[12] Mark Girouard, *The Return of Camelot: Chivalry and the English Gentleman*, (New Haven: Yale UP, 1981).

[13] "Wake," in *The Oxford English Dictionary*, (2nd edition, 1989), 827.

[14] Ibid. 828.

[15] Cambridge: Cambridge UP, 1981.

[16] Sharon Turner, *The History of the Anglo-Saxons, with a Vindication of the Genuineness of the Ancient British Poems*, 6th ed., 3 vols. (London: Longman, 1836).

[17] "Graft," definition 2, in *The Oxford Dictionary of Natural History*, ed. Michael Allaby, (Oxford: Oxford UP, 1985).

[18] Andrew Wawn points out, in *The Vikings and the Victorians* (Cambridge: D.S. Brewer, 2000), that "in the end, Hereward serves his defeated people better in death, as songs about his heroic life and resistance cheer his remaining followers in forest or fen, while they wait for a change in their fortunes" (319).

Participants in the 18th International Conference on Medievalism

Paul Acker: ackerpl@slu.edu
Lesley Allen: laallen@students.uiuc.edu
Lex Ames: amesav@slu.edu
Marjon Ames: marjonames@hotmail.com
Shellie Banga: scbanga@ucdavis.edu
Marilynn Board: board@geneseo.edu
Kristin Bovaird-Abbo: kbovaird@ku.edu
Eric Bryan: bryanes@slu.edu
Mark Burde: mark.burde@yale.edu
Christa Canitz: canitz@unb.ca
Alice Chandler: ChandlerAK@aol.com
Grace Chan: gcchan@students.uiuc.edu
Peter Christensen: petergc@csd.uwm.edu
Mary Davidson: mdavidso@ukans.edu
Deirdre Dawson: Dda1789@aol.com
Jason Delo: mightyd@uwyo.edu
Geneva Diamond: genevad@ku.edu
Carola Dwyer: cwdwyer@uiuc.edu
Bonnie Effros: beffros@binghamton.edu
Jennifer Floray-Balke: jbalke@ku.edu
Karl Fugelso: kfugelso@towson.edu
Rick Godden: rhgodden@artsci.wustl.edu
Tom Goodmann: tgoodman@miami.edu
Peter Goodrich: pgoodric@nmu.edu
Denise Griggs: denise.griggs.nshz@statefarm.com
Frank Grady: fgrady@umsl.edu
Curtis Gruenler: gruenler@hope.edu
Stefan Hall: halls@uwgb.edu
Kevin Harty: harty@lasalle.edu
Tony Hasler: hasleraj@slu.edu
Nick Haydock: NickHaydock@excite.com
Deborah Hyland: hyland@slu.edu
Michael Johnson: johnsom@buffalostate.edu
Graham Johnson: johnsogp@slu.edu
Philip Kaveny: pkaveny@mhub.facstaff.wisc.edu
James Keller: jrk@muw.edu
Keith Kelly: kellyak@slu.edu
Anna Kowalcze: anna_kowalcze@hotmail.com

Kathy Krause: krausek@umkc.edu
Elena Levy-Navarro: elena@jvlnet.com
Michael Livingston: lvst@mail.rochester.edu
Tom Madden: maddentf@slu.edu
Terri Major: tmajor@u.washington.edu
John Martin: jdmartin@ux1.cso.uiuc.edu
Becky Miller: millerbe@ku.edu
Gwen Morgan: morgan@english.montana.edu
David Murphy: murphydt@slu.edu
Michael S. Nagy: michael_nagy@sdstate.edu
Martha Oberle: maoberle@aol.com
Anita Obermeier: AObermei@unm.edu
Nils Holger Petersen: nhp@teol.ku.dk
Zina Petersen: zina_petersen@byu.edu
Jon Porter: jporter1@butler.edu
Tom Prendergast: tprendergast@wooster.edu
Jeremy Quartermain: quarterj@tcd.ie
Laura Reinert: reinertl@slu.edu
Sif Rikhardsdottir: srikhard@worldnet.att.net
Ed Risden: edward.risden@snc.edu
Keith Russo: KCRusso@v3mail.com
Henry Schilb: hschilb@indiana.edu
Sara Schwamb: schwambs@slu.edu
Tom Shippey: shippey@slu.edu
Clare Simmons: simmons9@osu.edu
Scott Smith: ssmith@nd.edu
Jenna Soleo: Jsoleo@gc.cuny.edu
Drennan Spitzer: drennanspitzer@hotmail.com
Alissa Stickler: ally0820@hotmail.com
Cindy Stollhans: stollhcj@slu.edu
Larry Swain: the swain@operamail.com
Jesse Swan: jesse.swan@uni.edu
Mickey Sweeney: msweeney@dom.edu
Paul Szarmach: szarmach@wmich.edu
Leslie Tannenbaum: tannenbaum1@osu.edu
Michael Teres: teres@geneseo.edu
Anne Thornton: hathornton@sbcglobal.net
Jane Toswell: mjtoswel@uwo.ca
Stephanie Trigg : sjtrigg@unimelb.edu.au
Richard Utz: richard.utz@uni.edu

Kathleen Verduin: verduin@hope.edu
Helena Waddy: waddy@geneseo.edu
John Walter: walterj@slu.edu
Rosemary Welsh: rwelsh@wells.edu
Richard West: west@engr.wisc.edu
William Woods: WoodsBill1624@netscape.net
Matt Yaple: mcyaple@hotmail.com

www.ingramcontent.com/pod-product-compliance
Lightning Source LLC
Chambersburg PA
CBHW070516090426
42735CB00012B/2801